NEW DEFINITIONS OF SCHOOL-LIBRARY SERVICE

NEW DEFINITIONS OF SCHOOL-LIBRARY SERVICE

Papers Presented before the Twenty-fourth Annual Conference of the Graduate Library School of the University of Chicago

AUGUST 10–12, 1959

EDITED BY

SARA INNIS FENWICK

CONTRIBUTORS

Francis S. Chase Margaret Hayes Grazier

Kenneth W. Lund Abram W. VanderMeer

Robert D. Hess Mary Helen Mahar

Jean E. Lowrie Sara Innis Fenwick

Frances Henne

21

THE UNIVERSITY OF CHICAGO · GRADUATE LIBRARY SCHOOL

THE UNIVERSITY OF CHICAGO STUDIES IN LIBRARY SCIENCE

The papers in this volume were published originally in the
Library Quarterly, January 1960

TABLE OF CONTENTS

INTRODUCTION

THE library institute held at the University of Chicago in August, 1947, was devoted to the various aspects of work with children and young people, the general theme being "Youth, Communication, and Libraries." Since that time the annual institutes and conferences have considered library work with young people only incidentally in connection with broader library problems, and not until 1959 was a Graduate Library School conference again devoted entirely to the needs of youth. Because the objectives of a library program designed for children and young people must be identified with the institution of which it is a part, the conference was focused primarily on the school library.

In recent years the process of evaluation in which educators and administrators are continually engaged received additional impetus from the general public. Changing conditions, increased pressures, and more urgent demands have forced a sharper look at the kind of education our public school systems provide. One thing that is becoming ever more clear is that the school library, at both elementary- and secondary-school levels, has a vital part to play in supporting and promoting the aims of education for today and tomorrow.

The completion of a new set of standards for school-library service in 1959 was an event of major importance. These standards were developed by the American Association of School Librarians, working with representatives of twenty other educational organizations. They set forth the principles and goals of an effective library program and describe the basic requirements of its realization. This statement can make a contribution to enriched learning only if all members of the community are committed to their implementation.

The Twenty-fourth Annual Conference of the Graduate Library School was devoted to a consideration of the role of the school library, with the hope that it would help to clarify future needs of school libraries. The sequence of papers in this volume was designed to orient participants, first of all, by a critical evaluation of educational goals and by pointing the direction in which school programs are moving in response to changing needs and objectives. New insights about the audience that the school library serves were reported in recent research in the area of adolescent problems. Another group of papers moves from the background area of edu-

1

cation in general to deal specifically with the school library's role—examining the implications of the new educational goals, the materials with which the school library must deal if it is to serve as an instructional materials center, and its relationships with the federal government and with public libraries. The final paper deals with the need for standards of excellence in library service and with the planning necessary to meet them.

The closing paper of the 1947 institute, by Frances Henne, was entitled "Frontiers of Library Service for Youth." These frontiers still exist for school librarians. In the last decade much progress has been made toward achieving equalization of library opportunities for youth, implementing the objectives of library service as developed by professional and accrediting associations, improving national, state, and regional planning, and developing the interpretative services of library work with young people; much, however, remains to be done. The papers presented at the Twenty-fourth Annual Conference together with the discussions they stimulated suggested challenging new frontiers. Increasingly, school librarians are being called upon to bring new and vital conceptions of their potential role in the education of youth.

SARA INNIS FENWICK
Conference Director

AMERICA EVALUATES ITS SCHOOLS

FRANCIS S. CHASE

THE topic "America Evaluates Its Schools" suggests three important questions. The first is whether the topic as stated is a just and apt description of the current attitude of the American people toward their schools. The second is, if so, what are the conclusions on which there begins to appear to be agreement with regard to the schools? And the third, and by far the most interesting, is what kind of image of the school is emerging from the kind of evaluation that is taking place?

At the moment I am inclined to give an optimistic answer to the first question, although it is still not clear that the appraisal will be sufficiently penetrating and inclusive or that action on the findings will be sufficiently decisive to present the characteristics of a great society re-examining its goals and re-constituting the means to attainment of what it most cherishes. It does seem to me, however, that viewed in the perspective of the post–World War II period the posture of the American people with respect to their schools has become more constructive in recent months.

THE PROGRESS OF EVALUATION

The debate on education in the period around the beginning of the present decade threatened to degenerate into a reckless attack on the schools, countered by an equally undiscriminating defense by school people. Then around the middle of the decade concern over the looming Communist threat and the demonstration of Russian supremacy in the field of space projectiles and satellites appeared to arouse a somewhat hysterical response to real and alleged weaknesses in education. From that time forward, however, constructive forces have predominated. Criticism has become more responsible and more discriminating; educators have begun to assume their appropriate roles as leaders of needed educational reconstruction; and public opinion appears to be crystallizing behind a comprehensive program to strengthen the schools.

The American people have always been critical of provisions for education. Throughout our history there have been more or less continuous efforts to measure education and the work of the schools against the needs and aspirations that arise in a free and adaptive society. The development of the American high school was the result of such an evaluation followed by new commitments on the part of the American society. Out of these new commitments came the resources necessary to house and instruct a high-school population that increased from 80,000 in 1870 to nearly 7,000,000 in 1940 and a college enrolment that rose from 52,000 in 1870 to a million and a half in 1940. What I am trying to say is that the present period of evaluation of schools and other means to education represents not a discontinuity in American history but a reassertion of tendencies deeply imbedded in our society.

The decade between the close of World War II and the mid-fifties can

3

be variously named, according to the tendencies and developments that one is emphasizing; but I think it is not a falsification of the record to think of it as a decade of American complacency, or, if you like, of rest and complacency. As a people we had been engaged in a taxing war from which we had emerged not only victorious but apparently as the foremost power in all the world and as the leader in the democratic traditions which we believed were destined to sweep the world. It was a temptation to equate the victory with the triumph of the American way of life and to conclude that there was no necessity for any serious re-examination of our basic institutions.

In this period a few voices warned that the noble aspirations, which in this country assume the name of the American dream, were far from fulfilment and indeed were perhaps in greater danger than ever before. Some of these prophets directed their scrutiny to the schools. Robert M. Hutchins was not entirely unheard in his cries against vocationalism and the intellectual disembowelment of American education, and other critics attracted momentary attention; but the American people were not stirred, and schoolmen were not deterred from pursuing the quest of an education addressed to conditions no longer dominant in American life. The notion of the good life had been confused with a notion of a safe, soft, and easy life. This, in turn, led to a concept of an education for happiness sought through adjustment rather than through achievement.

Many of the early critics were stronger in rhetoric than in logic and certainly more devastating in attack than they were effective in constructive proposals. Some, overlooking the obvious fact that

the schools so far from being unresponsive to public opinion had perhaps been far too responsive to the moods of the moment, attempted to lay upon teachers, school administrators, or teachers' colleges all the sins of commission and omission of the American society. To the extent that these critics offered solutions, they tended to find them either in our own past, in some other country, or in some never-never land of their own composing. Even Hutchins seemed to long for a time when knowledge was all of one piece and of manageable dimensions.

In the late 1940's and the early 1950's the field seemed to be pre-empted largely by a group of noisy and often irresponsible critics. But, at the same time, there were thoughtful voices raised, not in an attack on the schools, but in a call for re-examination of the premises of our society and for a reconstruction of education to meet new conditions. Responsible action, too, became more evident. In 1949 the National Citizens Commission for the Public Schools launched a concerted action "to help Americans realize how important our public schools are to our expanding democracy, and to arouse in each community the intelligence and will to improve our public schools." In this effort the Commission was joined by the Congress of Parents and Teachers, which slowly shook off its mood of acquiescence with established practice to assume a more dynamic role. Gradually, the demand for better schools gained in many segments of our society.

By mid-1950 it was clear to all thoughtful observers that the battle was not between those who wanted to destroy the public schools and the staunch defenders of American educational traditions but between the forces of inertia and those of constructive and orderly change. The real question began to be seen, not as "Have our schools deteriorated?" or "Are they better or worse than the schools of some past period?" but, instead, "Are our schools staffed, equipped, and directed so that they may adjust themselves effectively to the new demands now being spelled out by advancing knowledge, a surging technology, and the spreading aspirations of men?"

The appraisal of our schools, which seemed to be off to such an unpromising start in the late forties, began slowly to take more constructive shape. The launching of Sputnik dissolved the remainders of American complacency. The great foundations began to turn their attention to the needs of education for all age groups; the federal government began to exhibit an interest, first, in the production of scientists and engineers and, belatedly, in a wider range of educational needs. The debate was carried on avidly in the newspapers, periodicals, through radio and television, and into every community in the land. The great educational organizations gradually withdrew from their bomb shelters and began to exhibit, although somewhat timidly, leadership for the improvement of schools. The universities tardily recognized a share of responsibility for the whole process of learning.

For the present, however, it must be said that there is only a dim and partial perception of the gigantic task involved in reconstructing our schools to take account of new knowledge and new technology and the vastly enlarged dimensions of the educational task. Not only is the magnitude of the task not clearly apprehended but the planning is still partial and unimaginative; and the resources for achieving the needed reconstruction are not yet forthcoming. The obstacles to wise planning and effective action to bring about desired improvements in education are of several kinds. First, in spite of recent advances in psychological theory and research, our knowledge of how learning takes place is still sketchy. Second, there is as yet no general agreement as to the aims of education or the objectives to which the schools should address themselves. These two barriers, however, have always been with us and to a greater or lesser degree will always confront us. A far more formidable obstacle lies in the political area. It is made up of the thousands of small, ineffective school districts; is buttressed by archaic state policies in the fields of taxation and revenue collection and distribution; and is further augmented by a false and misleading tradition as to the relationship of the federal government to education. These political obstacles are not so formidable that they could not be resolved by vigorous and imaginative political leadership on the part of the President of the United States and the governors of the several states, with the assistance that a clear call in the interest of education would quickly rally to their support.

I hope, therefore, that it is not unduly optimistic to conclude that the movement is toward an evaluation that takes account of the multifaceted problems with which the schools must deal, assesses realistically the unmet needs for education, and pushes steadily toward better solutions than are now in use.

EMERGING CONCLUSIONS

In attempting to summarize the conclusions that appear to be emerging from America's evaluation of its schools, I shall weigh as best I can the impact of such governmental action as the passage of the National Defense Education Act, the reaction of citizens and professional educators to such widely publicized pronouncements as the Conant report on the high school[1] and the Rockefeller report on *The Pursuit of Excellence*,[2] and other indicators of public opinion. Yet I must confess that I probably am giving more weight to my own subjective assessment of the needs for education than to evidences of public demand. With this forewarning, I offer the following conclusions to the wary reader.

The direction in which America's evaluation of its schools seems to be leading is a new determination to see that all who can learn acquire a thorough command of the basic tools of learning, that access to the substance of a liberal education shall be brought within reach of a majority, and that effective inducements to lifelong pursuit of knowledge and meaning shall be kept before all citizens.

There appears to be increasing acceptance of the view that our schools must be credited with substantial contributions to American unity and to every notable American achievement, but that provisions for education fall dangerously short of the needs of our society at the present moment. To be more specific, I think the current evaluation is revealing five things:

1. Expectations for achievement in our schools have been set too low. The current temper is that more should be expected of children and young people and that the higher expectations will help to provide motivation to higher achievement.

2. The content of instruction is often outmoded, poorly selected, and secondrate. In some schools the content in physics, chemistry, and the other sciences reflects concepts so out of line with current theory as to produce unscientific, if not antiscientific, biases. The content in literature and in the social studies often does not provide the best possible insights into human behavior and achievements or into the evolution and effects of social institutions.

3. Mass-production techniques with standardized units of content through which groups of learners move at a uniform pace result in a waste of talent that is now intolerable. The waste occurs at both ends of the ability scale and, in fact, at every point where an individual is forced to curb his pursuit of learning to stay with the pack or is pushed ahead so that intelligent participation for him becomes impossible.

4. A shortage of good teachers and failure to make effective use of available teaching talent are handicapping learning in our schools. There are four aspects here: the failure to attract a sufficient share of our abler young people into teaching careers; the unimaginative and often deadening process of teacher preparation; the failure to make full use of, and to reward, the relatively few highly creative teachers or to differentiate the teaching task to take advantage of specialized abilities of many kinds; and the failure to extend the effectiveness of teaching through provision and appropriate use of a variety of technological aids.

5. The support of education is so far

[1] James B. Conant, *The American High School Today* (New York: McGraw-Hill Book Co., 1959).

[2] Rockefeller Brothers Fund, *The Pursuit of Excellence* (New York: Doubleday & Co., 1958).

from adequate and school organization in many cases so faulty that we have to re-examine all the premises on which we have been operating. It is my own conviction that a careful re-examination will point to more assumption of responsibility for financing on the part of the federal government and greater state responsibility for the creation of school units of adequate size and scope but that it will at the same time indicate the desirability of greater autonomy for schools so that each faculty becomes responsible for creating optimum learning opportunities for the population it serves.

I do not mean that all Americans accept all these conclusions. I do mean that those who have looked into the situation most carefully and a substantial number of those who have listened to the debate and read some of the reports are moving toward such positions as these. Now, if that conclusion is correct, what will happen to the schools? What is the new shape of things to come?

THE NEW IMAGE OF THE SCHOOL

Well, what is the old image of the school? I do not want to present a caricature, but, when we think of schools, what do we think of generally? We think of a building with a number of classrooms of uniform size; we think of teachers talking; students sitting passively, sometimes reciting, arranged in groups of twenty-five, thirty, forty, or whatever the mode is in a particular school; classes changing on the bell in high schools, and the day chopped up in smaller fractions in the elementary school; and promotion at a set time, whether it is annually, semiannually, or quarterly. The school tends to be a conveyor-belt system, moving everyone forward at predetermined rates. The so-called homogeneous or ability grouping plans modify the system only slightly, because, while the rate and content of learning may differ slightly among the groups, the individual within the group—and the range is still very, very wide—still moves at the predetermined rate through the predetermined content. Under this image of the school, learning is equated with teaching, teaching takes place in groups of standard size, and the school is administered in such a way as to standardize procedures in spite of all the obeisances made to individual differences.

The emerging image of the school is still blurred, but some of the ways in which it will depart from current practice are discernible. It will focus on learning rather than teaching and use teaching not so much to impart knowledge as to stimulate and guide learning. The school will become an organization functioning to bring together a large variety of inducements to and resources for learning and to create situations through which learning progress can be motivated, systematized, and appraised as far as possible on an individual basis. Its aims will be more sharply defined and will emphasize cultivation of the powers to search out and analyze ideas, to reach reasoned conclusions, and to identify with man's highest achievements and aspirations.

The aim in the primary learning stage is to keep active the child's inherent sense of wonder and to fit him bit by bit with the tools for pursuing the search for meaning through reading, observing, reflecting, identifying, enumerating, classifying, generalizing, and reporting. When he can make effective use of books to avail himself of the experiences of others in many times and places;

when he can use numbers as a tool in problem solving; when he is able to use the written and spoken language to pursue inquiries, to report what he has observed, and to set forth his conclusions, he is ready for the secondary stage.

Some learners will be ready for the secondary learning stage by the age of ten or even earlier. Others may not be ready before twelve; and some, because of special handicaps, may have to pursue essentially primary learning tasks even into adolescence under special provisions. The secondary stage or secondary school will be thought of as covering the entire period from mastery of the primary learning tasks to the beginning of study specialized to a life career. It should be a period of increasing independence in study and a period in which appropriate modes of inquiry are acquired for scientific, literary, historical, and other types of studies.

At all stages, contact with creative, inquiring, and well-stocked adult minds is essential; but, at the secondary stage, the need first becomes evident for the stimulation and guidance of scholarly specialists in particular systems of knowledge. Great minds can be met through books, and at times through films or with greater immediacy through television; but the role of the sensitive, alert teacher-scholar in continuous contact with the learner remains a crucial element. It is the teacher in the school who, with awareness of the learning potentials and needs of particular students, must provide access at the right times to what other sources can offer.

The library will become the major resource and center for learning activities. To carry out this concept, library functions and procedures must be redefined. The resources offered will include not only books in abundance but also microfilms, charts, recordings, film-strips, videotapes, and other materials to whet the appetite for learning and to feed the hunger for understanding. There will be special shelves easily accessible from which a student or a teacher may pluck a paperback edition of a scientific essay, a great novel, or a significant contribution to history.

The library with its auxiliary rooms will have accommodations for from one-fourth to one-half of the student population of the school. In secondary schools the library will be open for twelve hours or more a day so that students may pursue their individual inquiries before and after the regular school day and use it as a quiet place for study in the evenings. The central library will have easy access to cubicles for viewing and listening and small discussion rooms where students may assemble sometimes with an instructor and sometimes without. Moreover, movement of individual students between the lecture rooms, the laboratories, the shops, and the library must be possible without unnecessary red tape or an elaborate system of monitoring and checking.

The library staff will include at least one highly competent, well-trained librarian employed on a twelve-month basis and a staff of assistants with a variety of experience, training, and competencies. The librarians will conceive their task as that of helping students discover and use the knowledge in books, documents, recordings, films, and other records of human experience and observation. They will be aware of the learning objectives toward which teachers' efforts are directed and will share with teachers constantly their specialized knowledge of relevant materials for each type of learning. To facilitate this kind of interchange, a librarian may serve as a member of the curriculum planning group in each field of instruction. Librarians will also contribute significantly to guiding and evaluating student progress. To discharge these and related functions throughout the lengthened day will require a library staff of not less than three in a high school of two hundred students. For each additional two hundred students, at least another member should be added to the library staff.

To provide access to a rich content and context for learning is perhaps the most important single element in a quality education; but we cannot anticipate that either societal or individual ends will be well served unless there is intelligent guidance of young learners. There will be need for continuing appraisal of learning progress and a continuing effort to transform the child's search for meaning into systematic inquiry pursued for longer and longer periods on more and more significant problems through more and more sophisticated methods of study. The school is going to have to use a great deal of imagination and ingenuity in managing this process. It will succeed only to the extent that the primary learning stage is passed successfully without dulling the child's initial sense of wonder, and the extent to which the primary learning tools of reading, observing, using numbers, and so on, are acquired. With a good start, the student in later stages can pursue his own inquiries with increasing independence and at the same time sharpen and augment his learning skills while accumulating a body of knowledge which itself becomes a tool for further inquiries.

If we are wise, there will be no sudden and radical departure from established practice but rather a steady and vigorous movement toward more effective teaching and learning. Improve-ments in organization and procedures will be shaped by creative imagination and application of all that we have been able to learn through psychological and other research.

The measure of the school is the quality of the experiences provided and their appropriateness to the development of the particular individuals concerned at given times. The response of the pupils is the acid test, and relevant questions are: How many exhibit a consciousness of self-value, a sense of achievement, and a commitment to the pursuit of learning? And is there any increase year by year in the proportion of those whose achievements match their capacities and any corresponding decrease in the proportion who respond to the school's demands with manifestations of defeat or with adaptations requiring little effort and promising little growth?

The emerging school will have heightened expectations for its members. It will offer a content rigorously selected with regard both to the worth of the ideas embodied and to their probable influence on the development of particular learners at particular times. It will encourage each individual to move at his own pace toward goals appropriate for him. It will hold before him many inducements to learning, especially the inducements represented by contact with scholarly and inquiring teachers and with the ideas found in great books and other records of human achievement. In all it does, the school will seek to awaken a wish to know and a will to use knowledge for the common good and will exercise intelligence and imagination in providing more and more effective means toward the achievement of these aspirations by more and more of those with whom it deals.

NEW DEFINITIONS OF EDUCATIONAL GOALS

KENNETH W. LUND

MOST of us are frightened when confronted with the word "new." There is a security in old practices and old beliefs. There is a threat implicit in a recommendation for change, as it infers a criticism of the present and of the current group of practitioners, and it calls for venturing into the unknown and often untried, with opportunity for failing and feeling foolish. Not a pleasant prospect.

However, there is no question that we are in a time of great potential for change in education and that educators cannot rest on the concepts of the past to plan for the challenge of tomorrow. It is with this sense of urgency that I have agreed to think with you about "where we are and whither we are tending" (to paraphrase Abraham Lincoln).

The accelerated pace of change in our times has been so well documented in modern professional literature and mass media that it needs no lengthy treatment here. In brief, the world-wide population explosion; the revolutions in the techniques for harnessing physical energy; the incredible technological changes with importance for space, for communication, and for industrial procedures—all remind us that the world of today is to be supplanted by a radically new world of tomorrow. Our educational program preparing young people for world citizenship and for effective vocational and personal contributions in this world must be carefully planned if the challenge is to be met. Unquestionably, this education must have depth and quality and must prepare young people for maximum flexibility in meeting new situations and new responsibilities.

However, we should not accept the changing times as proof that we must change the goals or purposes of education. We have some time-honored educational goals in American education. We are part of the oldest public education system in the world—a quite remarkable fact when we recognize our newness as a nation. Today other nations are following our commitment to serve all the children of all the people. The other nations of the world are recognizing the crucial role education plays in shaping the destinies of nations and of free men. To be certain that we all appreciate the significance of this philosophy, may I share with you an experience of one of my friends during the second World War.

He was stationed in New Guinea during the early days of the war and was experiencing one of those quiet periods so common between combat episodes. One Sunday four of our officers, including my friend, took a PT boat and went up the river to shoot alligators. A short way up the river they drew near a sand bar and noticed a native woman seated in the sand, with child held in her arms and seated between her legs. They pulled the boat over toward her and called to her several times but could get no response. They were puzzled at the unusual situation but pushed on up the river for their recreational outing. Some three hours later when they returned the tide was high and the sand bar had disappeared. The woman and the child were gone too.

Two days later my friend had a chance to discuss this experience with a British missionary who had been in the area for many years. The missionary was distressed at the story and showed a reluctance to discuss the incident, but my friend persisted. Finally, the missionary explained with great emotion that this was a native practice to eliminate the diseased members of the tribe and that this woman undoubtedly was found to be tubercular. Her child was sacrificed, also, to guarantee the extermination of the disease. This was the accepted way of safeguarding the group— by sacrificing the individual. "One life is worth so little in their eyes," was the comment of the missionary as he ended the discussion. It is against the background of other cultures where human life is cheap that we can learn to value the true strength of our own.

In essence, the first and foremost concept which undergirds the American educational system is the sacred worth and dignity of each individual. As a corollary it is of paramount importance that we find ways to serve him with the optimum educational program and not some compromise that neglects or even stifles the unique potential he possesses. There have been some in this heyday for critics who have questioned the wisdom or even the possibility of continuing our efforts to reach all the children. To them it would seem wiser to conserve our intellectual and fiscal resources by spending them on the most apt individuals, with little or no concern reserved for those whose talents are limited. I am sure that you already sense my own bias in this respect.

In this sense I would suggest that there is a need for a rededication to an old concept—that each child is entitled to the best our society can offer and that this should not be limited by fiscal barriers, by the limited vision of educational practitioners, or by archaic governmental constitutions or legal restrictions which prevent the appropriate mobilizing of society's efforts to realize these goals. These goals must continue to include the transmission of our cultural heritage, the development of an enlightened and informed electorate, the mastery of skills and the development of attitudes for effective human relations, and competence in communication skills adequate for a rich life in a dynamic world. It will include an opportunity for optimum self-realization and the acquisition of skills for making a significant contribution to society. It should include a quality of personalized service through guidance that will aid young people in solving problems and evolving constructive personal plans and becoming purposeful individuals. These, as I see them, are the major goals of American education. They are not new, but are in danger of being lost unless some new methods are found to achieve them.

During the last two years since Sputnik there have been four documents of great significance, produced under diverse auspices, all calling for public action to make it possible for American education to achieve its goals. These documents are listed in chronological order of their appearance:

1. The Educational Policies Commission. *The Contemporary Challenge to American Education.* Washington, D.C.: National Education Association, 1958.
2. The Rockefeller Brothers Fund. *The Pursuit of Excellence.* Garden City, N.Y.: Doubleday & Co., 1958.

3. James B. Conant. *The American High School Today.* New York: McGraw-Hill Book Co., 1959.
4. The President's Science Advisory Committee. *Education for the Age of Science.* Washington, D.C.: Government Printing Office, 1959.

All these documents are alike in calling for a greater public effort to support education in a manner to make a high-quality program possible. All recognize the inroads on quality that have been made by decades of depression, war, and neglect. It is apparent that the time is right for educational improvement if the leadership of the profession is ready for the challenge.

It was Victor Hugo who said, "Greater than the force of marching feet is an idea whose hour is come." The idea of *quality education* is now having its hour, and in the decade ahead it is up to the professional educators in the field to demonstrate the vision and the competence to capture and direct the enthusiasm and the desires of the American people, channeling the efforts for effective action.

But what type of action? Is there a recognizable pattern or trend discernible today and likely to claim our interest and support for the days ahead? It would be a bold man who could claim to read the signs of the times, but I would like to offer some thoughts which you may or may not accept as you plan for your school-library programs.

First, it is apparent that we are being called upon to re-examine our values in American life and their importance for education. There are current signs of concern for and emphasis upon *intellectual excellence.* For some time we have seemed to stress the importance of equality and fairness in the treatment of all. It is apparent that society and schools

are now mobilizing to achieve an insistence upon quality and distinction. This concept of excellence will embrace many kinds of achievement—perhaps as many as fourteen types of giftedness, as identified by Jacob W. Getzels and Philip W. Jackson, of the University of Chicago. It will stress excellence without depreciating the moral worth of all. It will encourage great achievement, not at the expense of others, but as a service to society and to self. It will mobilize the rewards and incentives of society so that great attainment is appropriately recognized. In the words of the Rockefeller Brothers Fund report:

> We believe that man—by virtue of his humanity—should live in the light of reason, exercise moral responsibility, and be free to develop to the full the talents that are in him.
>
> Our devotion to a free society can only be understood in terms of these values. It is the only form of society that puts at the very top of its agenda the opportunity of the individual to develop his potentialities. It is the declared enemy of every condition that stunts the intellectual, moral and spiritual growth of the individual. No society has ever fully succeeded in living up to the stern ideals that a free people set themselves. But only a free society can address itself to that demanding task.[1]

Second, there is some evidence that the American people and educators are going to accept *the reality of individual differences* and support efforts to do something about them. For more than a century our educational literature has abounded with discussions of individual differences and the need for differential methods of organization and instruction. Yet today the majority of our classrooms are organized in heterogeneous groups, with little more than a courteous nod to

[1] The Rockefeller Brothers Fund, *The Pursuit of Excellence* ("Special Studies Project Report V, America at Mid-Century Series" [Garden City, N.Y.: Doubleday & Co., 1958]).

the wide range of differences in each group.

In short, the facts of individual differences are startling and have been well known since 1900, with the work of Binet and his followers on the measurement of intellectual capacity. Children entering school differ by four years in mental age; by middle grades their differences in capacity and achievement range from six to eight years; and by high school these differences are even greater although no longer accurately described by the age-grade index. However, although no one can question the facts as portrayed here, there is still much reluctance among educators and the public in accepting, for example, Dr. Conant's recommendation that we have ability grouping in English, mathematics, and science classes and in others where possible.

It is essential that we now implement the principles of ability grouping, acceleration, and enrichment of instruction for all with the aptitude for handling challenging material. The research in the field of acceleration is clear, and the advantages are obvious. It is possible to shorten the period of schooling, save time and money, avoid social and emotional maladjustment, develop some work habits, conserve national manpower, and increase the chances that the educational program of the individual will continue to completion and to the full realization of intellectual potential and service to society.

In spite of the clear answer coming from educational research, both educators and parents have been loath to accept the premise that acceleration is in order where circumstances warrant it. Perhaps we need to re-examine the reasons why we are reluctant to speed these talented youngsters on their way. In the main they are delightful to have around, and their parents enjoy keeping them young and dependent. In truth, teachers would be glad to pass along the nuisances quickly if they could but are quite possessive in retaining the gifted for as long as possible.

The research in the area of ability grouping is less clear. However, it is believed that this is primarily because grouping is meaningless unless a different type of instructional procedure, different course content, and revised standards of attainment are set. In general, the experience with ability grouping seems to indicate that teaching a group with a lowered range of ability permits greater breadth and depth, more time for creative and stimulating activities, and a more significant level of student contribution through individual experimentation and critical analysis. In addition, students develop better work habits; and as they learn to compete, they develop more realistic self-concepts.

It follows that ability grouping can make possible these improved learning experiences, but they will occur only where the instructional leadership is competent and takes advantage of the possibility. This implies a new approach to teaching, to be subsequently discussed.

The advanced placement program is deserving of special mention because of its dramatic growth and significant impact on American secondary education. It has been common to scoff at the slowness with which new ideas gain acceptance in educational practice. However, this program is truly an exception. It began in 1954, when twelve public and six private high schools met in a conference with some of the selective colleges and agreed to experiment with teaching college-level work in high schools to carefully selected and highly motivated high-school students. From this modest beginning the program has grown each year until this last May some 570 high schools had more than five thousand students writing examinations which were scored under the auspices of the College Entrance Examination Board organization and forwarded to the university of choice for credit and placement.

Many university administrators have commented on the willingness, even eagerness, of their faculties to give full recognition to this work. Time does not permit further comment on this fine program, but a full account may be found in the December issue of the *Bulletin of The National Association of Secondary School Principals*. The development of this program to one of national significance in five years furnishes concrete evidence that the time is right to press for full recognition of exceptional intellectual talents and to make adequate provisions for them.

Third, there is evidence on all sides that we are going to have significant *changes in the curriculum* after many decades of little change. There are national commissions at work in the fields of mathematics, physics, and biology. There is a rebirth of interest in foreign language, with much emphasis on oral-aural techniques and the development of functional mastery of the language by offering additional years of instruction. There is evidence that entire university faculties are becoming concerned about teacher preparation, and we are moving toward the time when we can expect both subject-matter mastery and teaching competence from our public-school teachers. In some ways the changes in the curriculum field are the most remarkable, for our prejudices in this area

run deep. Ray Lyman Wilbur, former president of the University of Illinois and Stanford University, once said, "Changing the curriculum is like moving a cemetery. No matter how long what's there has been dead, it still has a lot of friends." However, there are signs that the sleeping giant is now aroused and that the chances for improvement in the decades ahead are excellent.

Perhaps a word is in order on the direction these changes are taking. From the Conant report comes a call for urging the academically talented students to take the "tough subjects"—four years of mathematics, four years of one foreign language, three years of science, in addition to the four years of English and three years of history and social studies required of all. Some have criticized the Conant report as superficial in discussing merely amounts of time to be spent in subject areas. It is obvious to me that Conant fully expects the highest quality of instruction within each subject area but speaks in terms of courses and years because that has become the educational "coin of the realm."

Within subject areas the work of the Commission on Mathematics of the College Entrance Examination Board group might be cited as the direction change will take. Their report is now available and represents three years of highly significant work. It highlights the national need for a larger body of mathematically literate people and notes the inadequacy of traditional algebra and geometry courses in terms of the full intellectual development of the talented. The Commission recommends a revised three-year sequence, with emphasis on such topics as sets, nature and use of variables, inequalities, deductive reasoning, coordinates, vectors, and complex numbers. It urges evolution rather than revolution but stresses the urgency of change. Similar reports are coming in other subject areas, and all will have implications for the instructional program of tomorrow.

Fourth, there are signs that we are ready to assimilate the findings of psychology and educational research and make significant *changes in our methods of instruction.* Procedures which depend upon the sterile, textbook-centered, rote memorization of facts seem to be on the run at last. As never before we are finding an interest in creative teaching, in developing critical and analytical powers in students, and in developing skills of exploration and intelligent inquiry. The self-contained classroom and single textbook gives way to the library, to the research project, to the study of issues, conflicting opinions, basic references, and skills of independent research. From this viewpoint the library becomes the heart of the teaching-learning situation, and the library staff members are key partners in developing a truly dynamic educational program.

This program of the library will have impact on the instructional efforts of the English, history, social studies, and foreign-language departments, but also it should serve science, mathematics, industrial arts, home economics, and other areas that have not traditionally been reached. As we move toward increasing emphasis on intellectual excellence, there is evidence that we need to upgrade our instructional efforts in these areas from the "how-to-do-it" level to the higher realms of intellectual pursuits, with the understanding of basic principles, concepts, and relevant historical foundations. A broader design for our libraries with adequate staff and materials is basic to this point of view.

Fifth, and last, there is much evidence

that we are facing a new day in *utilizing the products of modern technologies* to improve education. For a while we have seemed to doubt that radio, videotape, television, movies, overhead projection, audiotape, and slides were here to stay. As a profession we have more often chosen to resist their intrusions rather than to initiate professional inquiry into the potential value they have for increasing the intellectual attainment of students.

This year there are signs that the intelligent inquiry has started. The National Association of Secondary School Principals has published a monograph entitled *Images of the Future* which describes a new organization for a school, breaking with the traditional concepts of one teacher for each twenty-five pupils. The July issue of the *Nation's Schools* contains another version of the school of tomorrow.[2]

In some ways it is remarkable how little our schools have changed. Our modern schools would be the one place where a citizen of the nineteenth century could feel at home, as he recognized the familiar procedures and purposes. He might comment on the pastel walls or the plastic furniture, but the activities would be familiar. Yet it is through the intellectual power fostered by the schools that our advanced technology has flowered and developed. It is time we called on our technological leaders to plan with us the best possible use of these tools to guarantee a quality program for all children. We must commit to films, to television, and to the machine those tasks which are best handled by them. Then we must personalize student-teacher re-

[2] Kenneth W. Lund, "It's Time for a Breakthrough," *Nation's Schools,* LXIV (July, 1959), 43–45.

lationships in a manner to guarantee optimum quality.

A student in our program must receive the help he needs to develop the power of independent intellectual inquiry, the mastery of the necessary skills for handling reference materials and research and experimental techniques, and the ability to write and report on the results of his study. He will require individual help in library and laboratory; he will need small-group opportunities for discussion of issues, problems, and reports of his writing. He will sometimes be part of a large group, and at other times he will receive through television or film, the material best handled in this manner. It is time to discard our allegiance to the 25-to-1 pupil-teacher ratio in all subjects and for all types of activity. It is time for honest inquiry to determine the best methods and to encourage the implementation of the findings.

There is no question that we shall see some significant changes in the schools of tomorrow. Many of these changes will call for substantial increases in the financial support the public provides for schools. It is imperative that we approach this challenge as true professionals, interested in improving educational opportunities for boys and girls and confident that the stature of the teaching profession will grow as our quality of service is improved. It will be necessary for us to re-examine our current practices of how many students per teacher, of who should grade the papers, and of how we should handle the clerical and custodial aspects of school operation. Our development as a profession with stature comparable to the other great professions requires that we find the best answers to these questions—that is, best for the boys and girls we serve.

In every sense the era ahead promises to be an interesting one for American education. In no sense will it be a quiet one. For the fainthearted, one can promise no sanctuary. In the words of the Killian report it will be a time of "ferment, not chaos." Change must come, but it must be assimilated in orderly fashion, for our young people are too precious to be wasted while we delay or bicker.

Each of us in our professional roles has much to contribute to this great quest for a better program. The answers will come from many sources and will be attained through the increased effectiveness of each person practicing his profession with greater effectiveness. It is to this cause we should pledge ourselves and our full support.

THE ADOLESCENT IN SCHOOL

ROBERT D. HESS

ADOLESCENCE as we know it in the United States is virtually unknown in most societies throughout the world. Although there are rumblings that come from observers' reports and the news services that the turbulence we associate with teen-age culture in the United States is spreading into urbanized, industrial sections of Europe, South Africa, Japan, and Australia, this country still offers the most obvious demonstration of adolescent storm and stress. However, it is not the exhibition of crisis and conflict alone that gives American youth culture its unusual features. As a subculture, as a period of personal experience, and as a defined phase of psychosocial development it contrasts with adolescence in other parts of the world. I wish to consider, first, the place of adolescence as a part of American society; second, the central conflicts and crises of adolescents as individuals; and, third, the meaning of the high-school experience for the teen-ager.

Perhaps the most prominent and significant feature of adolescence in this country is the fact that it has become such a visible and dramatic part of the social system. The impact of youth culture upon adults comes in part from the vigor of teen-agers and in part from the strength of numbers. Teen-agers number approximately seventeen million, a figure that will swell to twenty-four million within the next half-dozen years. This is a group not only vocal as individuals but one that has public representatives speaking for it through maga-

zines, motion pictures, television, recordings, and newspapers. In dealing with teen-agers, adults are puzzled and uncertain. On the one hand, we devalue and even depreciate teen-agers; we dramatize and exploit their aberrations in the daily press, the monthly magazine, the theater, and television. We examine their problems in public conferences and in newspaper columns; we scream of their crimes in our morning headlines, but as a society we have not provided a place of respect and usefulness for them which can challenge their imagination and abilities. The teen-agers respond to both our condemnation and our confusion. They believe themselves underrated, mistrusted, and assigned to an inferior status. In a study which Irene Goldblatt and I conducted a few years ago we discovered that both teen-agers and their parents held false and distorted ideas about each other. Adults felt that adolescents were likely to overrate themselves and to overestimate their maturity; teen-agers actually, on the research instruments we used, rated themselves in close agreement to the ratings they received from adults. However, they indicated that they expected adults to underrate teen-agers grossly as a group and to minimize their maturity and sense of responsibility.[1]

[1] Robert D. Hess and Irene Goldblatt, "The Status of Adolescents in American Society: A Problem in Social Identity," *Child Development*, Vol. XXVIII, No. 4 (December, 1957). These data come from parent-child pairs of adults and teen-agers. For a more detailed account of the significance of the images family members hold of one

17

There has been, in this country, an increasing tendency to prolong the period of adolescence—that is, the length of time between puberty and the beginning of productive, or at least adult, roles in society. The initial signs and symbols of physical and social maturity appear with some frequency at the elementary-school level. The pre-adolescent often seems prematurely sophisticated and eager for adolescent heterosexual behavior. At the other extreme we have acted to delay the time the teen-ager can enter the labor market. This is accomplished both by legislation controlling the age at which an adolescent may accept employment and by the demands of an industrial society for highly trained technical workers and for post–high-school education. For various reasons, the decrease of gainful employment in the United States has been apparent since the early part of the century. As late as 1920, almost 60 per cent of boys sixteen and seventeen years of age were employed. By 1940 only half that number held jobs. The proportion had risen to 36 per cent in 1950, reflecting an expanding labor market. The decrease is more marked for adolescents under age sixteen and less so for those older. However, even in 1920, the proportion of employed was much smaller in this country than in countries such as Italy, France, and England, where, by age sixteen, approximately 80 per cent of boys were gainfully employed.[2]

The apparent rise in high-school and college marriages suggests that adolescents in their late teens are resisting this prolonging of pre-adult status. This seems to me to be an inevitable consequence of the lengthening of the teen-age period. If the teen-ager is urged toward maturity at an early age, we can scarcely be surprised if he refuses to remain docile and childish but occasionally grasps the prerogatives of adults before the adult world is willing to extend them.

The relatively long period of adolescence is complicated by a second feature: the ease of physical mobility, both in freedom to range far and with relative frequence and in access to means of transportation. The implication of this feature lies in its possibilities for extending the world of experience and in the ability to escape the supervision of adults. This relative freedom offers the adolescent more opportunities for making his own decisions on a wide variety of social and sexual matters. This is not to suggest that these decisions are necessarily unwise. It does suggest, however, that teen-agers have opportunity to assume responsibility over significant and potentially crucial aspects of their personal lives.

Not only do teen-agers have freedom of action but they also have at their command economic resources of remarkable scope and impact. The teen-age market is respected by industry. Clothes, phonograph records, books, and movies are but a few of the products which attract the billions of dollars which teen-agers spend annually in the United States. Almost five million teen-agers have part-time jobs during the school year, working after school hours and Saturdays as clerks, gardeners, baby-sitters, and extra help in markets, serv-

---

another and of the teen-ager in the family see Robert D. Hess and Gerald Handel, *Family Worlds: A Psychosocial Approach to Family Life* (Chicago: University of Chicago Press, 1959), chaps. i, iii, and v.

[2] See R. G. Kuhlen, *The Psychology of Adolescent Development* (New York: Harper & Bros., 1952), chap. iv.

ice stations, and at home. During the summer vacation, twice as many are employed. These are in addition to the three-quarters of a million who have full-time jobs. It is difficult to calculate the total income of teen-agers in this country, but estimates place the figure at approximately nine billion dollars a year.[3] This is in addition to the money spent on them by their parents. This economic power permits them to exercise a strong, perhaps dominating, influence over the popular-record industry, as we are painfully aware in the protracted contemporary reign of "rock and roll."

These three circumstances—a long adolescence, relative freedom of movement, and economic resources—contribute to produce the most distinctive feature of adolescence in this country—a teen-age subculture, somewhat apart from the main stream of society, which in a number of significant respects sets its own code of behavior. The trade mark of this subculture is its demand for differentiation from adult society and from the symbols of previous teen-age groups. The slang of the teen-age group changes constantly, so that the young adult is quickly out of touch with the peculiarities of verbal communication that he had so recently used to show that he was "cool," "hep," "in the know," or otherwise an up-to-date knowledgeable member of his group. The lines of influence among teen-agers are very strong as they attempt to keep pace with the crowd, but they are by no means divorced from the values of the society or from the constraints exercised by adults. A recent study by Brittain

indicates that, in the crucial decisions regarding ethical, moral, and career choices, they still tend to align themselves with the standards of adult society, while in matters of lesser consequence they disdain the old-fashioned manners and behaviors of their elders.[4]

Contrast this picture of American adolescence with that of an adolescent in Italy, described to me recently by a visiting professor from that country. There, in the typical instance, the boy is expected to complete necessary schooling by his early teens, after which he is apprenticed and expected to work full time. Childhood and adolescence, as we know it, both end abruptly and with little time for indulgence in the youth culture that he may occasionally see in American movies. His energies are more controlled, more directed, by the society, and his indoctrination into adult roles and behaviors comes relatively early in life.

How shall we evaluate the phenomenon of teen-age culture in the United States? It seems to me that a fair appraisal must view it not so much as a pattern of aberration on the part of our youth as a product of the complex society in which we live. We have greatly increased the devices of mass communication in the last three decades and have made these generally available to adolescents, providing them with a knowledge of the world and its problems and opportunities, stimulating them to new and adult-like experiences. At the same time, we have tended to give children and adolescents more freedom and have relaxed the strict moral codes of a half-century ago. We have taken them off the labor market and delayed the time

[3] For a brief summary of the economic power and habits of teen-agers see "Teen-Age Consumers," *Consumer Reports,* XXII, No. 3 (March, 1957), 139–42.

[4] Clay Brittain, "Parents and Peers as Competing Influences in Adolescence" (unpublished Ph.D. dissertation, University of Chicago, 1959).

when they could assume the privileges of adults; nevertheless, we have tried to contain, by social and moral sanctions, the dynamic energy of youth. Although we have tried to place the blame for their mistakes on every available object—the family, the teen-agers themselves, television, comic books, the cold war, the school, the church—we have yet to deal effectively with the problems that confront adolescents and, through them, ourselves. A description of the social characteristics of the adolescent period only hints of the meaning which this phase of life holds for the individual teen-ager. Although we may concern ourselves with the impact made by youth upon institutions such as the school, the corporation, or the church, it is the influence youth culture has upon the individual boy or girl that must eventually command our attention.

There are many problems which face the adolescent as an inevitable part of the period of growth and development he has reached. The obvious and natural fact of physical growth, of changing physical dimensions and features, of sexual maturation, and of the uncertainty about the final results of this physical redevelopment are in themselves sources of anxiety, or pride, and often shame and tears. We have made this aspect of the transition to adulthood particularly stressful by creating national standards of physical beauty that can be achieved by a disappointingly small proportion of our population. Coming to terms with physical resources that cannot be changed by diet, cosmetics, plastic surgery, the gym, reducing salon, or hairdresser is certainly one of the important problems which the adolescent meets. So must he also learn to make his way with his peers,

to be unafraid to stand up and be counted, and to adopt a code which, whether deliberately or not, dictates his behavior. These problems, however, are insignificant in comparison with the central problem of American youth—a problem that we have largely created for ourselves and our children: the task of finding and maintaining a sense of personal social identity.

The concept of personal identity, and here I am drawing from Erik Erikson's excellent definition and discussion, is a condition of mental and emotional well-being which is represented in two areas: first, the individual person's sense of continuity and stability in his definition of himself and, second, the recognition of this individual person's identity and worth by the community of which he is a part.[5] Identity implies individuality and reciprocal respect between the person and his peers; it means being recognized rather than unknown and respected rather than ignored. The opposite of identity is role diffusion, the feeling of uncertainty about one's place in the larger group or inability to commit one's self to an occupation or to a lasting relationship to another person.

Identity derives primarily from two sources: sex-role identification and commitment to an occupation or career. Both these areas of behavior define a man or woman's place in the community, determine many of the significant details of personal life, and often dictate the cultural and social and economic levels in society in which they may be accepted. The development of a sense of individuality and of self-respect is founded upon these two central areas

[5] Erik Erikson, "The Problem of Identity," *Journal of the American Psychoanalytic Association,* IV (January, 1956), 26–121.

of psychosocial behavior; they represent integration into a recognized segment of the society and permit the infinite variety of individuated versions of occupational and sex role that we have come to associate with individual personality. A society that presents a definite and unambiguous pattern of sex and career roles has little difficulty with identity and role-diffusion problems. In such societies children know at an early age the general routes to adult roles and the behaviors which will be expected of them eventually in the future. The choice of career is limited, and the position each career pattern holds in the society is evident. Our society, however, has a great number of highly complex, often contradictory, adult roles from which the teen-ager must choose. Standards of achievement, of moral behavior, of family responsibilities, and of personal excellence vary from group to group in the society. The great number of alternatives which we offer to our youth provides perhaps the most perplexing identity problems.

Our eagerness to be democratic parents, to help the teen-ager achieve his independence, and our own uncertainties in an era of great social and political change leave the teen-ager without clear direction, except that we keep him in public school, which might help organize his energies and direct his attention. In addition, he must grapple with the difficult problem of settling upon a course of action and commitment which will eventually lead to adult career. The complex set of roles offered by the adult society and the lack of adult direction combine to make the formation of identity one of the most critical issues of this age period. A sense of drifting, of pointlessness, of living for the immediately

gratifying are frequent experiences of adolescents, typified best, perhaps, by the contemporary phenomenon known as the "beat generation." It should not surprise us that they turn to each other for identity in groups, clubs, and gangs and are drawn to personalities who dramatize their problems through the mass media. The need to rely on the group to establish identity accounts for the popular tendency of social cliques, to the delinquent and non-delinquent, to give the group a name as a sign of solidarity to themselves and to their non-group peers.

The complexity and ambiguity of role behaviors possible in our society apply to sex as well as occupational roles. The emancipation of women and the freedom they have won to compete with men in a large and expanding number of fields have created role uncertainties for women and in turn for the men, who recognize the change in women and find traditional attitudes toward them no longer quite appropriate. Part of the complexity of role behaviors follows from the fact that there is relatively little consensus about behaviors and standards among the adult community. Within the same social group and along the same city block there may be patterns of behavior that range from strict, puritanical attitudes to casual acceptance. The force of the parent's example is blunted by the examples of other adults. Yet, at some stage in his development, the teen-ager must take on his own set of ethics and acts and identify himself with one of the many possible alternatives open to him.

The process of establishing an identity or of dealing with the identity crisis is essentially one that the teen-ager must complete for himself. No matter how much the adults around him may try to help, the final commitments, the subtle weaving-together and integration of all the elements that make up his personality, must be achieved by the teen-ager himself. Identity formation is a task of the ego and cannot be relinquished to an outside authority without serious threat to the autonomy of the individual person.

In an ideal situation the high-school experience would afford the adolescent with opportunity to deal with both of the central strands of his identity crisis —sex role and career commitment. To a degree this is possible. However, several factors tend to emphasize his pre-occupation with sex-role behaviors (dating, social facility, demonstrating masculinity or feminity, etc.) during the high-school period and de-emphasize or postpone the problems of occupational or career choice. Thus striving for popularity, interaction in social clubs, and the like are prominent aspects of the high-school non-curricular life. In moving away from the authority of parents and other adults and in experimenting with the behaviors which they consider to be more "grown up," they turn to each other for support, for information, and for rules of approved behavior. They often relate to institutions, as the church or school, in these groups or cliques rather than as individuals. At school, church, YMCA, as well as in informal leisure activities, the cliques are the basic social units. The clique establishes, in part, the rules for social behavior, defining activities that are approved and those that are rejected. While the influence of the clique or gang is strong, it is probably less overwhelming than many parents fear. One of the uses that the teen-ager makes of the

clique is illustrated by the views that teens and their parents displayed in a series of interviews conducted by one of our graduate students in the Committee on Human Development. When asked about the relative merits of single or double dating, both teen-agers and parents agreed that they preferred double dating to single dating for high-school students. However, they gave discrepant reasons for this preference. The parents revealed an opinion that double dating tended to decrease the possibility of sexual activity on dates; the teen-agers seemed to be relatively unconcerned with this problem. To them the advantage of double dating was much less dramatic. As one girl expressed it, "When four people are along, it's a lot easier to keep the conversation going. At least one of them can usually think of something to say." Thus the concern of the teen-agers was with whether they could properly and adequately meet the demands of a social situation, and they depended on one another for assistance.

This portrayal of the tensions of adolescence suggests that the high-school period is a time of rapid and extensive learning, much of it completely outside the scope of the high-school curriculum. In fact, it may tend to reduce the interest and motivation for acquisition of academic knowledge. This may occur not only because the school is competing with other interests but because the social clique or group may, sometimes deliberately, adopt a casual attitude toward intellectual activity. One high-school senior that we interviewed expressed it in roughly these words:

The fellows in our high school are more or less divided into three clicks. First, there are those who like school clubs like the All-School League, who like to be school officers, and stuff like that. Second, there's my group, those who fool around all the time—the Aces, guys who belong to different boys' clubs. Last are a bunch of little sissy boys—the group who just comes to school to learn. Our group is more or less the most popular. All of us are crazy guys—kind of fun.

To get into my group, you have to have a good sense of humor, go out for some sport, fool around in class—get average grades, know how to make out with the girls, be sort of tough, be able to take care of yourself, and don't chicken out of a fight.

The social clique may also reinforce standards of scholarship and intellectual interests. In a high school where Professor Allison Davis and I have conducted research we have found that the clique or social club often had a formal or informal expectation of its members with regard to behavior toward the school in many respects. It tended to exhibit a characteristic way of reacting to the school authorities that varies from active co-operation to planned programs for irritating and annoying teachers who, for various reasons, had attracted the dislike of the group. Such behavior was typically viewed by the teachers as the misconduct of an individual when in reality it was the expression of a group. Discipline against the individual member was usually ineffectual because of the reward and support the individual member received from the clique. At the other extreme were cliques of students who prided themselves on their intellectual ability and promoted science clubs, chess clubs, and other mental endeavors. The attitudes of such groups are indicated by the remark of one-high school senior when asked if he intended to go to the prom. His reply was, "Why should I go to the prom? With the money I would spend, I could pay tuition for a semester at the state university."

The adolescent's school experience and his behavior in the social club as well are strongly influenced by the social class environment from which he comes. Whether it is the shadow of the slums or the privileges of the wealthy exclusive estate, the impact of social background intrudes upon the individual from his earliest moment. It extends or limits his intellectual stimulation, determining to a great extent the use that he will be able to make of his genetic resources when he becomes an adult. The social background and the family through which its influence is exercised upon the young child molds the mental and, to a degree, the emotional faculties which the child brings to the schoolroom. The lower-class child comes to the classroom from a world which is geographically narrow and intellectually barren. One of my students recently completed a case history of a lower-class girl who had lived on the South Side of Chicago for almost ten years but who had never in that time visited the downtown area or seen Lake Michigan. This is not an isolated example. The intellectual deprivation suffered by a lower-class child is almost impossible for the middle-class adult to comprehend. The preschool books and bedtime reading are virtually unknown. The range of ideas and the concepts for directing his thinking are limited to practical concrete situations and the immediate problems of maintaining an existence. In contrast, the middle-class child is urged toward intellectual experience and is taught to reason and to deal with words and concepts, both verbal and printed. He is rewarded for mental effort and interest. His work at school receives careful and anxious supervision at home, and he readily learns the importance of scholastic competition and achievement. The influence of social class extends outside the classroom to his social interaction with other pupils and with the school authorities.

In high school the effects of social background begin to determine clique and other social groupings.[6] Participation in the formal school activities is limited by recognition of social status, on the part both of teachers and of pupils. The enrolment in various high-school curricular programs shows social class differences, with the middle-class student preparing for college and the lower-class student avoiding college-preparatory courses in favor of technical training, commercial courses, or a collection of courses regarded locally as the least demanding of effort. For some students the foremost aim of effort in high school is to achieve graduation. For the lower socioeconomic groups, the non-college–bound population of the high schools, the values of a high-school education are but dimly understood, and in many cases the reason for continuing is not so much to learn as to complete a task which the community has set for him, so that he will not be penalized for the lack of a high-school diploma. Unable to see the practical application of the material he meets in class and aware of the low social status that he holds in the informal social system of the school, the lower-class child may drop out before graduation with apparently little provocation. Of those who drop out before graduation, about 70 per cent blame the school or the school curriculum.[7] This is not so much a criticism of the school as it is an illus-

tration of the view of education held by the lower-class child.

The competition between a job and continuing in school is a strong one for the lower-class student, especially as he considers his post–high-school plans. The present wage scale for skilled labor is such that the decision to go to college may mean for him the loss of several thousand dollars in earnings, in addition to the expense of college, and with little promise that a college education will place him in a substantially higher-income bracket. While there is no question that, on the average, the college graduate makes more than the worker with only a high-school diploma, there are many individual exceptions to this. While the decision not to go to college is a sound one for many high-school graduates, there is a considerable number who have the ability and who could finance a college education without serious difficulty who still have no interest in higher education of any sort. There are, each year, approximately 60,000 high-school graduates in the upper one-fourth of academic ability who do not go to college; another 95,000 begin college who will fail to graduate.[8] A careful examination of the attitudes of teenagers (and perhaps their parents) toward the educational system and toward education itself raises serious questions about the status of intellectual effort and formal schooling in our society.

What does all this have to do with

---

[6] See B. Neugarten, "Social Class and Friendship among School Children," *American Journal of Sociology*, LI, No. 4 (January, 1946), 305–13.

[7] Harold J. Dillon, *Early School Leavers* ("National Child Labor Committee Publication," No. 401 [New York, 1949]); Elizabeth S. Johnson and C. E. Legg, "Why Young People Leave School," *Bulletin of the National Association of Secondary School Principals*, XXXII (1948), 14–24.

[8] Robert J. Havighurst, "Discovering and Motivating Scientific Talent," an address given at the St. Louis meeting of the *American Association of School Administrators*, February 24, 1958.

the library? From my position of relative ignorance about library science and the practical problems of library management, I can borrow indulgence and comment freely.

The first thing that impresses me is the incompatability that exists between the image of the typical library and the image of the typical teen-ager. Libraries in general are models of middle-class orderliness, docility, restraint, and courtesy. The library card is a symbol of intellectuality, of responsibility, with a touch of civic interest thrown in. Teen-agers present a picture of impulsiveness, lack of order, casual regard for responsibility, and a notable lack of respect for adult restraint. Whatever the term "square" means to a teen-ager, I am sure he would often apply it to most people on both sides of the librarian's desk.[9] I do not know what image the teen-ager has of the library and the librarian (and this is a point on which some useful research might be done), but from what we know of the teen-ager's attitudes toward adults and adult institutions it seems highly probable that it represents to him an extreme in adult restrictions and taboos on his typical modes of behavior. In addition, habitual and unnecessary trips to the library will rarely add to his status and acceptance among his peers. In contrast to the library are other sources of reading material available to him. I refer to the elaborate newsstands of urban areas and even of relatively small towns, to

the book sections of some museums I have seen, and to the magazine sections of the local drugstores. Here he has relatively easy access, a great deal of color and dramatic display, a feeling of excitement and adventure in fantasy, and little pressure for proper behavior and conformity to the regulations of an institution. The library is geared to the behavior and manners of adults and well-behaved children; the newsstand, the book section, and the pocket book display are tolerant and inviting. The library is designed, in part, to protect books; the newsstand is designed to excite his imagination.

If we were to plan a library center with the teen-ager and his youth culture in mind, what might be the features of such a place? I can imagine libraries or extensions of libraries—reading and communication centers, perhaps—located near community recreational facilities which would be designed for children and adolescents, with the underlying purpose of attracting the teen-ager to the book or magazine and making them accessible to him with as little red tape and formality as possible. One might consider a facility which would include, in addition to a central area for reading materials, motion pictures (adventure, sports, current history, natural history, professional advice, and many others), records (both popular and classical), tape recordings, video-tapes, and other permanent records of mass communication. The philosophy of such a center would be to stimulate reading and the acquisition of information and vicarious experience across a range of mass communication from popular culture to the classics. I believe that teen-agers would respond

[9] These remarks are intended to apply primarily to the *voluntary* use of public and school library facilities. They may seem inappropriate to persons accustomed to dealing with college-oriented, middle-class teen-agers whose home experience has encouraged reading and intellectual activities. They are particularly appropriate, however, to the situation that obtains for millions of adolescents from lower socioeconomic backgrounds.

with an enthusiasm that would astonish their elders and could incorporate such a center into their image of contemporary youth culture. Teen-agers want to read and to experience the unknown and the familiar through fantasy provided by the array of devices at our disposal.

I scarcely need to add that reading and other fantasy experience can be a means for the teen-ager to learn both about himself and the outside world and so can assist him in the effort to meet successfully the crises of his chronological age and the historical era into which he was born. We cannot obscure the fact that he is headed into a complex and often contradictory adult world; we do him no favor by shielding him from the realities he is about to meet. It is more communication about people, about the society, and about the world that he needs. The adult world and the library as a central institution of communication can help him in his search for a sound, productive, and creative social and personal role in the community.

ELEMENTARY-SCHOOL LIBRARIES TODAY

JEAN E. LOWRIE

MY FIRST experience as an elementary-school librarian, barely fifteen years ago, was in the community of Oak Ridge, Tennessee, where we all had a share in helping to create the new and, to some, frightening atomic age. Within this short space of time, we have plunged into another age—the space age—which has brought greater, perhaps more baffling but certainly more challenging, problems to society today. Among other things it has precipitated the elementary-school program into a whirlpool of conflicting educational arguments and, more specifically, has confronted the librarian in the elementary school with an entirely new group of materials, new approaches to teaching, and new curiosities on the part of the children. It is at this juncture that the elementary-school librarian now must evaluate his program and, in a sense, justify his existence. Either the services must continue to become more vital and important to the education of our children or the library will have no further reason for being.

The elementary school of today is predicated upon the idea that all children, regardless of their native ability, should be encouraged to pursue knowledge as far and as fast as their background, interests, and intellectual potential will permit. The cultural heritage of the world belongs to all children. The freedom to explore nature, to become acquainted with beauty in all forms, to enjoy the best in literature, to understand the past and in turn relate it to the present—this is the inherent right of every child. Toward this end the school curriculum and, more specifically, for our purposes, the elementary-school library program are conceived. The selection, the availability, the organization, and the distribution of materials gathered together in the centralized library is designed to be of use and value to the kindergarten child and the sixth-grader, to the teacher and the administrator, to the gifted and to the slow learner.

But the pace and character of modern life have complicated this basic purpose of the library. Questions are asked which relate to the scientific knowledge of our youngsters, to their ability and use of the basic skills, to the needs of the gifted child, to the lack of foreign-language comprehension, and to the area of the humanities. Are our children acquiring an education in these fields? Such questions are pertinent to the planning within the elementary school and influence directly the selection of materials and the scope of the program of the elementary-school library.

The picture is an optimistic one, however, for a study of today's elementary-school programs, as they are presently emerging in various sections of the country, indicates changes which are the result of the current trends in educational thinking and the new impetus from aroused concern of laymen. A closer examination of some of the exciting features becomes important, for

27

it presents proof positive of the flexibility in organization and the availability of all materials in today's elementary-school library. The patterns which are being developed are evidence of the co-operative working and planning of teachers, librarians, and administrators, which is, after all, the basic key to good library service.

Let us consider first of all the materials which are to be found in today's elementary-school libraries and the philosophy behind the organization of these media. Technological progress has directly affected the library world. Many mechanical aids in the field of audio-visual service have been introduced to the teacher. They provide variety in teaching techniques which are useful. But these same media now present information in more popular vein which is accessible to the elementary boys and girls outside the classroom. Unfortunately, the body of knowledge which these devices emphasize is often of a superficial quality and encourages the acceptance of statements at face value. It is here that the classroom teacher and the elementary-school librarian must work closely together—to capitalize on the interest aroused in order to expand the child's curiosity into new areas of thought. For, if the elementary school is to become truly the preparatory program for secondary and higher education, the introduction to new meanings and new ideas, the first steps in learning to draw conclusions from varied sources, and the acquaintance with our rich cultural heritage must begin in the kindergarten and primary years of school and continue throughout the entire educational program.

It is the responsibility of the librarian therefore to select materials which will challenge the intellectual capacities of the gifted child and will encourage the slow progression of a reluctant reader. These materials will be books, magazines, pictures, pamphlets, films, filmstrips, slides, recordings, and other graphic materials, and they will be easily accessible to all members of the school population. For this instructional material is expendable. It is to be used. Youngsters come in to listen to recordings for a dramatization or story, to seek information for a classroom unit or to listen for fun; to preview filmstrips in the individual viewer for a committee assignment; or to search for pictures to interpret a report for the classes. This is in addition to the constant use of books for all these purposes. Furthermore, the organization is not on the basis of first-, second-, or third-grade level. Rather it is organized to capitalize on the interests of all students both in curriculum enrichment and in reading for pleasure.

A glance at the utilization of library materials in two broad areas should further point up the expanding services which the librarian is quick to give in new and old areas of interest. In the broad program of social studies in today's elementary school, many areas of life are included. Historical and geographical concepts are taught. International, interracial, and interreligious understandings are developed. Modern community life is studied from the familiar city helpers in the first grade to international government in a sixth-grade unit. The concepts of democracy and other ideologies are presented in order that intelligent decisions may be drawn. The librarian thus must be prepared to guide children to information in any or all of these categories—within the planned unit or for the individual seeker of information.

Among the concepts presented in this field, one finds a definite emphasis on the heritage from the past and its present-day implications. It may be pioneers and the West, with its tall tales and stories of hardships, or ancient and medieval civilizations and the inheritance of the ages. Reports which cover such topics as papyrus, picture writing, cuneiform, the printing press, Roman laws, Renaissance art, crafts, and guilds, and world religions are all directed toward learning how people of the past influence us today—in communication or labor movements, for example. Such diversified projects as taping a discussion on a chapter from *Web of Traitors* to give background for Greek civilization; or a group pantomime based on the "Twelve Labors of Hercules" may be carried on in one classroom simultaneously with the study of the industry, topography, and present-day social conditions of modern Greece. The sharing of favorite Greek myths by one group to coincide with the use of a filmstrip on gods and goddesses brought in by another committee, plus book reports on historical fiction titles from a different group, may also be included in this same study. This is all based on library materials and skills.

While these activities are in progress in one room, another class may be involved in a study of life in the hot, wet countries. A puppet show is planned which needs background music of the Congo or South American jungle, and the library's record collection is searched. Pictures of animals, homes, and customs must be located. Stories are provided for background reading and may in turn lead to creative dra-

matics as one form of sharing the information.

In building collections of science materials within the library grade level is not the only criterion for selection. The librarian purchases books on dinosaurs, rockets, or electronics which will be of use to a first-grader or to an eighth-grader or to both. Frequently, schools do not use a specific science textbook, and then the research must be done entirely through library materials. Special topics require many sources. Encyclopedias may be examined; the card catalog is used; the unabridged dictionary gives definitions; the vertical file is combed; the index in the science book must be checked; and even the science-fiction books prove of value.

As an example of diversification in science one may find that, while a fourth-grade room is studying trees, seeds, and flowers in the fall, the teacher is sharing excerpts from a biography of George Washington Carver and emphasizing his interest in plant experimentation. This simple unit may thus include a valuable contribution in the humanities and develop a better understanding of the relationship between science and human welfare.

The tremendous interest in the International Geophysical Year also sparked a definite library quest. This was an area where little up-to-date information was available on an elementary level, so the librarians were forced to do real searching to satisfy the curious primary youngster as well as the boy in the sixth grade who had quite mature understanding of the problems facing such projects as "Operation—Deep Freeze." The influence of Sputnik was immediate and obvious, but the interest which it engendered in weather and atmospheric conditions, stars and planets, day and night, seasons, etc., went far beyond the sphere of physics and rocketry. Here, too, the kindergarten teacher as well as the junior high teacher needed material for his own background and to help interpret the developments of scientists. Librarians were confronted with an enormous job in coping with this crisis.

Correlated work in health and safety, art and music, as well as in basic arithmetic skills, are implemented through library materials. Safety, fire, and conservation study is aided by vertical-file and audio-visual materials for current information. Exploring bypaths can lead to the use of such books as *Superstitious? Here's Why, Microbe Hunters, Tune Up, The Wonderful World of Mathematics,* or *Minn of the Mississippi,* depending on the particular interests aroused in the group.

The librarian therefore must be a participant in the curriculum development within the school. She must have an understanding of the teaching approach used by the classroom teacher and be alert to all opportunities to enrich the classroom program. It follows also that, if young people are ultimately to become self-sufficient in locating the sources to answer their questions, functional library instruction must become a part of the teacher-librarian planned program.

The library instruction program which is planned to acquaint the entire school with the possibilities of the library must be a most flexible affair. Its over-all objective is to stimulate and encourage enthusiastic use of all libraries (school and public) through an informed handling of their resources. The general program which outlines the desirable learnings that an elementary-boy or girl should possess before going into a junior or senior high school is

planned by the librarian and has been based on the needs and requests of teachers and students over a period of years. But the specific lesson on a particular tool or skill is dependent upon the immediate need of the individual or group. A formal lesson in the use of the card catalog, for example, is usually presented at the request of the classroom teacher and in direct connection with a unit of work in the room. When the children have discovered that they must know how to find many materials for class reports, they look for a tool which will aid in organized searching. Thus the card catalog becomes important to them. This need usually develops in the fourth grade, where the urge to gather additional information is strong. On the other hand, there are many third-graders who are capable of understanding the use of the simple card catalog and are anxious to find books by themselves. A good librarian capitalizes on both of these possibilities —the classroom need and the individual curiosity—and two methods of instruction are followed.

This is an aspect of elementary-school library service which requires close teacher-librarian co-operation. Some teachers prefer to present the parts of a book, the techniques of note-taking and allied skills in connection with the language arts programs. Others prefer to have the librarian introduce the skill or tool, with classroom activities planned to reinforce learnings. The significant point, however, is the break from the traditional prescribed list of skills to be learned in each grade in the direction of a presentation according to the needs of the particular library and its public, the interests of the children as excited by their own curiosities. Meaningful presentation results in more enjoyment in the use of library tools. The value of an organized arrangement where children easily learn to locate materials is immeasurable and is obvious, for the library must be constantly tapped in all phases of learning and becomes an extension of the classroom.

Reading guidance in all its aspects is an equally significant part of today's elementary-school library program. It may mean sharing of books and stories through the story hour in the library, or it may involve work in the field of teaching individual reading. It may expand reading interests beyond the narrow confines of "Another dog story, please," or it may stimulate creative dramatics and writing.

Sharing stories aloud, stories which present stimulating new worlds and evoke the imagination, is one vital aspect of reading guidance. But the stories which are presented, the books which are shared, must arouse an excitement for further exploration in recreational reading. These materials are not chosen merely for the value in curriculum co-ordination, an animal story because the room is having a unit on animals, beneficial as this experience may be. Rather it is shared because Little Georgie in *Rabbit Hill* is excitingly written and worthy of being shared with all children. The vividly dramatic Norse myths, such as "How Thor Lost and Found His Hammer," are presented not because one is studying Norway and must correlate stories with social studies learnings but because the freshness of another culture's traditional literature, its concept of the ancient world and its thunder-god, has an appeal to the imagination of the child and provides for further understanding of the close relationship of all men. The selection of such material demands the maintenance of literary standards as the number-one criterion. The correlation to curriculum enrichment is of secondary consideration.

The introduction of good literature is a basic consideration in the entire educational program. Fairy tales, myths, fables, poetry, classics, and fine modern writing all appear in the library collection. They are good antibiotics for the inane, often poorly written stories of modern life which appear in many text and trade editions. Discriminating taste and recognition of sound writing can be developed in informational reading as well as in leisure reading. Furthermore, the plethora of informational books now being published makes it possible for the school librarian to evaluate all books for literary values as well as for accuracy and unbiased presentation of facts.

Individual reading guidance has been an important aspect of the elementary library program for many years. But the trend toward individualized teaching of reading in the classroom involves a new use of library books and new techniques of service by the librarian. This program is predicated upon the availability of a large collection of books on many reading levels and of varied interests. It is necessary for both teacher and librarian to work closely together in guiding the individual reading choices, choosing the books to be used in the classroom, and providing supplementary materials. It necessitates that the librarian be conscious of each individual child's ability; that she help him to be aware of the fact that reading is pleasure, not drudgery; and that books may be read both for individual delight and for the satisfaction of personal curiosity. More and more teachers are using library books for the teaching of reading to supplement or replace the basic text which all must read "before passing." Such a program helps the youngster to move along as rapidly as he is able to rather than limiting him by the group's personnel or the book itself. Many of the new books which we have today are inviting in both appearance and content. They are exciting and imaginative and may be read by the beginning reader as easily as the traditional "See Puff run." Teachers who are using this method for the teaching of reading are united in their belief that it is absolutely necessary to have a good library before embarking on such a program and a librarian who is interested in developing this new technique.

With the current emphasis on foreign languages, the movement to teach a language other than English in the elementary school has received great impetus. Here, too, the library plays a significant role. Many European children's books—picture books, fairy tales, and stories—are now available in the United States in the language in which they were originally written and published. Delightful picture books are coming from our own presses which present basic French or Spanish phrases and conversation aids for the beginning language learner. More and more story books, as well as non-fiction titles, which present accurate, well-written descriptions of boys and girls in these same countries, help to bring about a better understanding of customs and speech and add to the broader concept of racial and world understanding so necessary to the future existence of all peoples.

The elementary-school library has its own particular contribution to the needs of the accelerated or gifted pupil. This is another area which has currently been receiving special attention from educators, parents, and interested citizens. Schools where special programs have been developed for these superior learners must have available materials which will constantly stimulate exploration into many areas and attempt to answer at least some of the questions posed by the children as a result of wide reading. These accelerated readers, avid seekers of knowledge, need variety and depth in their reading material. The children with special interests and abilities in science need more detailed, more advanced information than the average youngsters. The library presents an opportunity for the child to explore on his own. It offers a time and a place for face to face conversation about books. It allows for the wide reading necessary when text prepared materials are inadequate.

Gifted children need to be kept busy constructively, and the library is the laboratory facility which provides this opportunity. These children also require special guidance in the area of recreational reading. More often than not their direct interest is also their recreation. They make much use of reference materials, but they need introduction to other interests, particularly in various forms, to literature. Whether these programs are carried on in the regular classroom or whether there is a special provision for this group, the elementary-school librarian is ready to secure the books which will be needed and to assist in the expanded use of the materials.

The slow learners are not forgotten in the special services area, however. Displays of easy and picture books are prepared for class visits to the library. Many easy books are loaned to the classroom for the express purpose of arousing an interest in stories and encouraging the effort to read simple material independently. Books, filmstrips, and pictures which help in the teaching of the practical—food, clothing, shelter needs, newspapers, health and safety areas—are made available. A teacher checks out special airplane books for a second-grade problem child; a group which can be challenged by simple biographies of explorers and pioneers finds satisfaction in the library; a nine-year-old boy in the first grade becomes a library helper. These are experiences which may be found in elementary schools where the librarian is sensitive to the problems of this particular group.

Librarians are also experimenting today with programs for the physically handicapped as well as the mentally retarded children. Youngsters who are able to attend school despite these handicaps are encouraged to participate as far as possible in the total school program. They serve as good library assistants, even though they may arrive on crutches or in a wheel chair. Work with sight-saving classes as well as with totally blind children is carried on. Books with large print, talking books, and books in Braille are a basic part of the collection in schools where these boys and girls are encouraged to be with their peers in the regular school program. Librarians also serve the homebound children by sending collections of reading materials for both pleasure and information with the visiting teachers for distribution as needed. The concern which society feels for these special groups is mirrored in the diversified planning of the elementary-school librarian.

The interest in reading skills engendered by controversial articles, lay discussions, and professional queries has further implications for the librarian. Elementary-school personnel are waxing enthusiastic over the increase in skills, vocabulary, and comprehension, as seen in the reading-test scores. Administrators and reading consultants are frank to say that very often this may be due, in large measure, to the development of a *good* library program within their schools. Such results underscore again the need for a trained librarian—one who can give the service necessary to arouse latent abilities and produce an interest in reading which will become paramount in the lives of young people.

On the periphery of this basic program in curriculum and reading guidance, one discovers other trends in today's pattern of elementary-school library service. The opportunities are present in the elementary-school library for student assistant programs and for the organization of a library council. Youngsters may help before and after school or perhaps during the noon hour. They offer assistance when primary classes come to the library and, of course, are of great help when their own room is in the library. They are the ones who help out when the librarian is called from the room, who card books, paste, shelve, and do many of the routine tasks. Occasionally, boys and girls are excused from the classroom to help during the teaching day. This is done when their classwork is completed. Generally speaking, however, the program of teaching in the elementary grades today precludes the use of released time for regular library assistance during classes. Therefore, the librarian encourages their help at other stated times. Most of the student library helpers are alert, active, and eager users of library materials. They serve as valuable liaison people between the library and the classroom. There are special instances when youngsters with problems are encouraged to help in the library. It may be simply the need for a job with responsibility—a chance for the child to prove that he can be of service to the school. It may be a child who is a slow reader as compared with the rest of his room who has thus become a behavior problem and needs the special encouragement of leisurely browsing, without pressure, to discover his book interests. The entire program is planned in such a way, then, that it will not exploit the child but rather help to develop library skills. Worthwhile experiences can be provided only in situations where the librarian has time to guide and to supervise the children. Pride in achieving a high standard of work even though routine, the development of the sense of responsibility, and practice in library skills are all potent arguments for further expansion of this facet of librarianship in the elementary school.

In elementary schools where experiments are being carried on in camping programs or in extended summer programs, the librarian follows through with additional materials and changes in routines where necessary. Library materials may be shared with children's rooms in public libraries to supply additional materials, or, if the school has its own summer activity classes, the librarian presents story hours, circulates books, and generally encourages the continuing program of reading during vacation months. One elementary librarian even went to camp with a group of youngsters in order to know how best to make library resources applicable in this experience! Background reading for the camping experience as well as materials which will be of value in the actual program itself, such as community living, out-of-door life, and nature study books, are provided.

Services which relate directly to the teacher and his problems become part of this over-all framework. The problem of obsolesence in our rapidly changing technical world is one which influences the library directly and necessitates a specialized service to teachers. Children are far better prepared for this space age than the teachers, and they continually subject the teachers in the elementary schools to many questions which are often beyond their ability to answer. There are questions on technological processes, on nuclear energy, on rockets and missiles, on electronics, and on Antarctic exploration which completely baffle the classroom teacher. In the elementary school where one teacher is responsible for the entire academic area of work, it is necessary that there be provided sufficient materials on these subjects. The youngsters themselves may be referred to this, but, even more important, these materials offer a clear, basic explanation or answer to the questions which the teachers ask and which provide a background for further study for them. Such new and exciting books as the handsome edition of *The Sea around Us* or of *The Wonderful World of Music,* which fill in the forgotten or neglected areas in the teacher's education in both science and the humanities, also serve to stimulate further exploration on the part of the children.

In addition to this, another aid for teachers which has developed within recent years is the growth within the individual elemenatry-school library of professional collections—books and magazines which are needed by the teacher as he searches for answers to behavior problems, methods to make the acquisition of skills meaningful learning experiences, or research in special educational fields. A vital expanding program develops when the needs of all members of the school population are adequately provided for.

The elementary-school library is developing physically in response to demands of the expansive yet concentrated total school program. It now demands space adequate for housing individual, committee, and class groups simultaneously. It requires space for the storage and distribution of many types of materials. It has become an instructional materials collection which is centrally located and is so functional and so flexible in its operation that it may be used in the classroom, at home, or in the library for long or short periods of time. This library presents an atmosphere conducive to browsing or study, to satisfy individual and classroom needs. All this demands the services of a full-time professional librarian—one trained in library techniques, in educational methods, with an understanding of child growth and development. This plus reasonable clerical assistance will provide the basis for a program such as has been depicted above.

An over-all review of the role of the elementary-school library today would not be complete without a look at what should be changed and what should be retained—the strengths and the weaknesses.

It is evident that the kind of program which has been described cannot exist in situations where the scheduling of classes to the library is so restricted that no one may come into the library except at his particular time, once a week or even every other week. A situation where the scheduling cannot allow flexibility of teaching and the concomitant use of the library, or where the librarian is so afraid that someone

may disturb her story-hour group that she locks the library door whenever a class is inside, defeats the purpose of the entire program. Granted that it is desirable to contact all children regularly, but, when the schedule becomes paramount and the service secondary, a modification is necessary.

It is unfortunate also that many elementary-school librarians or teacher-librarians retain too tight a control of the library materials. The fear of wide circulation of materials outside the library or of the development of the autonomous classroom collection rather than the fluctuating collection has deterred the program in elementary-school library service. Books and pictures should be available in such quantity that there will be a sufficient number for simultaneous use in the library or in the classroom as further expansion of the unit of study.

And then there is the librarian who talks about "my" library, "my" books, who does not let the teachers make suggestions about the material needed for teaching, or who sends the children away from the desk because the records will be all mixed up. If the library is to justify its existence, it does so on the service-to-all basis. This means that it is public domain, and the student and the teachers help in planning the program and enriching the collection. Unfortunately, there are also administrators who believe that the library must be administered as a traditional classroom program. Lesson plans must be devised for each period of the day with no deviation. Tests are administered regularly. The library becomes a formal situation. Children are restricted to library visits only after all their work is finished, or, worse yet, the library is a detention room, and a child is sent there only if he cannot behave in the class group. This is a way of thinking which is evident in far too many schools and calls for a revaluation of the function of the library in that school in terms of administration and services.

The scope of service must be increased to all the children in each elementary school. The library is not the sole property of the youngsters who can read. It belongs alike to the kindergarten child who is just being introduced to the delight of many picture books, to the second-grader who is still struggling with pre-primer material, and to the fifth-grade child who is pursuing a reading program which is designed for a slow reading group. The enjoyment of books and the delights of reading plus the understanding of the library as an information center begin to develop with the youngest child in the school program. The library must be open to serve all. Where programs are planned only at the third-grade level or above, re-examination of policy seems important.

Inadequate budgets and untrained librarians in the elementary school must be removed from the picture of the future. It is useless to purchase large quantities of materials and then have no one who can adequately organize and distribute them. It is equally poor planning to attempt to maintain a library on the pittance gifts from the PTA or fifty cents per pupil. The current tendency to employ a teacher "to keep" the library one or two periods a day is unfortunate. It is impossible to offer a vital functional library program without a person trained in the methods of library service and who is available to the school personnel at all times.

But there are exciting trends which should be emphasized and expanded. The professional elementary-school librarians with their fresh and enthusias-tic approach to all the interests which arise in the school community deserve encouragement. There are many such people, but more are needed. Materials which stimulate the creative, imaginative thinking of the child, arouse the scientific interest and awareness of search, stimulate the ability to draw one's own conclusion, present the cultural heritage and help one become aware of world relationships are the kinds of materials which may be found in the active, vital elementary-school libraries today and which should become a reality in all.

There is now apparent also a centralization of facilities, such as cataloging, processing, and sharing of special materials, which will increase the ease with which much can be made available to many. Again on the positive side of the ledger is the increased provision of time for free reading and independent study in the library for teachers and pupils alike. The awareness on the part of the librarian of the special needs within the individual school as well as within the entire educational movement promotes the type of service which excites the enthusiasm of co-workers. The growing awareness of the classroom teacher and of the administrator of the existence of the library is contagious. The enthusiasm on the part of teachers who have experienced this library program is inspiring. Teacher, librarian, and administrator cooperation is one of the great strengths which help to promote the educational program as pictured for today's child and tomorrow's adult through the library. The elementary-school library is proving to be an exciting development in the total education movement today as well as an essential requirement of all elementary schools of the future.

IMPLICATIONS OF THE NEW EDUCATIONAL GOALS FOR SCHOOL LIBRARIES ON THE SECONDARY LEVEL

MARGARET HAYES GRAZIER

THE librarian must know what school men see in their crystal ball to envision the school library of the future. If they be false prophets, then any librarian's concept of the future library is likely to be dismissed as the illusion of an overenthusiastic zealot. On the other hand, if the school men prove sound oracles, the school library must alter its contents, staff, quarters, and administration to fit the new program.

I make two assumptions in visualizing the high-school library of the future. First, the library should emphasize tasks that are particularly appropriate in contrast to those that are best done by other departments of the school. Second, the library will make no distinction about the form of materials it will administer. Television, radio, disk recordings, tape recordings, films and slides, mock-ups, models, and museum materials will be found with the traditional books, magazines, pamphlets, and pictures. After all, if the newer media had existed at the time of the codex, libraries might not have been called "libraries."

KINDS OF MATERIAL NEEDED IN THE FUTURE HIGH SCHOOL

Teachers and students will expect more from the library. Teachers will not only prepare materials for class but will also be expected to assist in planning curriculum and do research. It is likely that they will have more time in the school day and the school year for their study; many will be employed on an an- nual basis and will need the library during the summer as well as the winter. Able students will be enrolled in several of the college-level advanced placement classes offered in all academic fields. Science, mathematics, literature, and social sciences, required of all students, will have special courses for those who cannot write and read well enough to succeed in college preparatory classes. Students going to work immediately upon graduation will study part of the day in technical and vocational classes. All pupils will spend some time in arts, crafts, and music classes.

The demands of teachers and students will affect both the content and the form of the library collection. Teachers will expect the library to have the basic professional journals, yearbooks, and bibliographies in their special fields. Superior students in advanced placement classes will require college-level books and journals. Students with reading and language handicaps will need simple readable printed material for social science, science, and literature courses as well as the specialized journals and handbooks essential for their technical and vocational training. There will be newer instructional media for all classes: disk and tape recording for foreign-language laboratories; prints, slides, and recordings for art and music classes; film, filmstrips, and tapes for slow readers in general education classes. All materials will be loaned to classrooms and laboratories for as long as needed, but additional copies will be available in the

37

library for the use of students there.

The future library will also have an important role in the production of instructional materials needed in the school. The staff may tape radio and television programs, school band and orchestra concerts, and important speeches and dramatic productions for later use by classes. Students, teachers, and library staff will use library workrooms to make slides, charts, posters, maps and diagrams. In schools with proper equipment, the library staff may assist in producing films and filmstrips. Since preliminary reference work in the library is necessary for making most new instructional material, the library will assist in production indirectly as well as directly.

SELECTION AND ORGANIZATION OF MATERIALS IN THE FUTURE HIGH SCHOOL

In my survey of proposals for the future high school I found frequent mention of what the student is supposed to learn in school. He should understand methods, principles, and major concepts in each field and be able to apply them to practical problems. This shift in emphasis from facts and information to analysis and understanding places new demands upon the library. For example, it takes a more sophisticated library collection to answer the question, "Why is the crime rate higher among lower-income groups?" than to compare the crime rates of the ten largest cities in the United States. Similarly, the question, "What will be the effect of the opening of the St. Lawrence Seaway in 1959 upon Detroit and neighboring areas?" requires more from library resources than statistics of Michigan manufacturing during 1959. The fact that such materials may be needed by students who are excellent, average, and indifferent readers extends the quantities of materials the library must have to meet such needs.

The library staff in the future high school will have to devote longer hours to material selection than in the past. The wide variety of purposes and needs which materials must serve will require continuing study of critical reviews in journals and special selection aids. Teachers will assist in selecting materials, but the library must assume major responsibility for the development of the materials collection.

Although library card catalogs and bibliographies furnish a general analysis of the subject content of books and other non-print materials, they do not yield the more refined analyses of theme, idea, method, organization, and readability needed by tomorrow's teachers. The future high school will expect the librarian to give expert assistance in the use of materials. The librarian's expertise will be based on understanding of the methodology, concepts, and data in a given field and familiarity with basic materials for youth. He will study carefully the materials in his collection in terms of their possible uses. He may prepare catalog cards with more detailed analytics; he may make out special lists and indexes. He will *not* be the librarian whose primary contribution to curriculum committees is to turn the pages of the *Standard Catalog for High School Libraries* to note what books are included in the appropriate Dewey classification.

LIBRARY'S ROLE IN STIMULATION, INTERPRETATION, AND USE OF MATERIALS IN THE NEW HIGH SCHOOL

Traditionally, the school librarian has fed his professional ego by donning two pedagogical caps. He assisted the individual student to select books and other reading materials—in short, reading guidance—and he taught classes, groups, and individual students how to use the library. Both these functions evolved naturally from the library's primary responsibility for providing, organizing, and making accessible the printed materials needed in the school.

The concept of the librarian's part in reading guidance has been expanded in several directions. Librarians have realized that in even the small school they cannot guide the reading of each individual child. Many now advocate a school-wide reading guidance program in which teachers and librarians cooperate. Teachers are encouraged to spend time in class talking about books of general interest in their field that students might read for their own enjoyment—a mathematics teacher, for example, might suggest *Mathematics and Imagination* or *The Education of T. C. Mits;* a social problems teacher, *The Exploding Metropolis* or *The Hidden Persuaders,* a science teacher, *The Sea around Us* or *No Place To Hide.* Librarians assist English teachers in planning the voluntary or recreational reading aspects of the English program by recommending titles, preparing lists, and talking about books. Librarians believe that voluntary reading is important and that the curriculum should allow time for it. Some librarians have intensified their reading guidance activities by forming library reading clubs to review and discuss good literature.

Individual reading guidance in the library is no longer limited to helping pupils find materials to develop present interests and to foster worthy new ones. The guidance in reading guidance has been stressed. Books are used to help students solve personal, ethical, and vocational problems; librarians are encouraged to counsel pupils informally about their problems as well as locate helpful materials.

Buttressing this bibliotherapy is the personal influence of the librarian operating upon student library assistants. The library assistant program, originally conceived as an admittedly poor substitute for efficient help with the many clerical and housekeeping chores in library work, has been recently rationalized as an excellent way to help the personal and social development of students. Librarians praise the developmental values of the program as they invest ill-spared time in supervising an ever changing corps of helping hands. Many library leaders urge that the program enlist the bright, the slow, the physically handicapped, and the maladjusted. From this motley band, librarians hoped to interest a few in library work as a vocation, naïvely overlooking the fact that the sponsor operating all too frequently as a clerk and study-hall attendant is not a figure to inspire professional disciples, especially from among the brighter students.

What will happen to the library's mushrooming guidance programs in the future high school? The school's increased concern for the individual student—his varying abilities, interests, needs, and educational progress—is evident in almost all statements of educational goals for the future. Gilchrist predicts that each student will be a member of a basic instructional group, probably in the social science area, taught by a teacher who knows him and his family well.[1] Conant emphasizes the

[1] Robert S. Gilchrist, "Innovations in the High-School Curriculum," in Francis S. Chase and Harold A. Anderson (eds.), *The High School in a*

importance of tailor-made schedules for the individual student and the need for more guidance personnel in the high school.[2] Chase visualizes "a school unit or division open only to those who have acquired certain fundamental tools of learning and have demonstrated a capacity for study."[3] Counselors, or home-room teachers, will be important members of the teaching staff in the "new" school. Their function will be to know well what each student is able to do, to plan his schedule accordingly, and to evaluate his progress continuously.[4] Trump, on the basis of experiments now in operation, predicts revolutionary changes in the organization of instruction. Methods of teaching, student groupings, and teacher and pupil activities will adjust to the aims and content of instruction. Both teachers and students will have more time to meet individually or in small groups.[5] Current experiments in dividing larger high schools into smaller schools or houses are attempts to provide an organization in which the student does not lose his identity in the mass.

What are the implications for the library of this concerted effort to improve guidance in the high school? I predict

that the library will be forced to limit itself to an indirect role in personal, social, and vocational guidance. Its major task will be to acquire the materials needed by counselors and teachers for their guidance work with students. In short, librarians will be librarians and leave counseling to the counselors. Student assistant programs will be dropped. Clerks will take over the work of the student assistants; counselors will find an outlet other than library work to help students resolve personal and social problems.

The library's reading program will similarly emphasize assistance to the teacher in locating materials in all subject fields for slow readers, for gifted readers, and all the in-between varieties. Librarians will continue to co-operate in planning voluntary or recreational reading programs for English classes so that this important aspect of students' learning may be provided for. The library staff will spend more time in book talks before large class groups in all subject fields. Librarians will continue to help all students who ask for assistance in selecting books and to publicize new materials through displays, announcements, and lists, but the program will focus upon stimulating and assisting the teacher.

The library's role in library instruction has also undergone radical but less confusing change. Several decades ago such instruction was regarded as the responsibility of the librarian alone. Library instruction was quite cut-and-dried; textbooks were fairly well agreed about the basic skills to be taught and the appropriate methods and drills for teaching them. The librarian asked for a week of English class time to teach "the library" to freshmen or first-year classes. This was a simple but ineffec-

---

New Era: Papers Presented at the Conference on the American High School at the University of Chicago, October 28–30, 1957 (Chicago: University of Chicago Press, 1958), pp. 212–13.

[2] James B. Conant, *The American High School Today* (New York: McGraw-Hill Book Co., 1959), pp. 44–47.

[3] Francis S. Chase, "Making the High School a Place for Study and Learning," in Chase and Anderson (eds.), *op. cit.*, p. 190.

[4] *Ibid.*, p. 191.

[5] J. Lloyd Trump, *Images of the Future* (Urbana, Ill.: Commission on the Experimental Study of the Utilization of the Staff in the Secondary School, Appointed by the National Association of Secondary-School Principals, 1959), pp. 7–11, 19.

tive program, and there was considerable evidence that students neither liked nor remembered these formal and isolated lessons. There has been a growing belief that the most effective teaching is that integrated with the work of the classroom. The librarian and representative classroom teachers prepare an over-all plan and decide in which courses within broad subject areas the student should get to know certain library tools and reference books. Librarian and teacher then plan together the specific lessons in which it will be necessary for the student to use these tools. In addition to this program, librarians help teachers introduce relevant tools to class groups and review library skills whenever such instruction is deemed necessary by the teacher.

It is unlikely that there will be major changes in the general program of integrated library instruction. The increased use of library materials for the variety of purposes described in the first section of this paper means that the librarian in the future school will be familiar with what teachers are trying to teach and how library materials can help. This knowledge will enable librarians better to assist students in interpreting and using materials. Gone forever (we hope) are the days when hordes of students descended upon the library with no more instruction from teachers than "to look up the Supreme Court." The library will have its own self-teaching devices. Sound filmstrips operated by a push button will show the use of magazine indexes, the card catalog, and other bibliographical aids; disk or tape recordings will make available lectures by the staff on basic literature tools in various fields.

IMPLICATIONS OF NEW GOALS FOR THE LIBRARY STAFF

A reading of the new educational goals suggests at every turn a sizable increase in the amount of materials in every form that the future library will be responsible for. Building strong library collections and preparing intensive analyses of materials will require additional staff time. Eliminating superfluous activities such as student assistants and library reading clubs will free some time. The size of staff will be related, also, to the library's responsibility for technical and mechanical processing. Educators are vague in their estimates of requirements. They take refuge in such statements as " a corps of librarians will be needed." I suggest that the larger high school of five hundred or more will have a number of professional librarians and adult clerical assistants.

Positions in the new library will be based upon careful job analysis. There will be a clear distinction between professional and clerical assignments. Competent clerks will schedule, distribute, process, and repair materials. Such tasks as evaluation and selection of free and inexpensive material and preparation of bibliographies will be recognized as requiring specialists' knowledge and no longer assigned to students or clerks.

Larger schools will require some kind of subject specialization. Collections will be divided into the broad areas commonly found in some university libraries—humanities, sciences, social sciences. Personnel directors will be instructed to employ a science librarian or a fine arts librarian rather than simply a high-school librarian. Subject librarians will select, organize, and supervise *all* forms of material within their special areas; they will join what librarians and audio-visual specialists have put asunder. The need of larger schools for technical assistance in producing materials and using visual and electronic devices may justify special positions on the library staff.

Those librarians wishing to do so will work on a year-round basis and will be paid for their additional service. Many high schools will offer summer sessions for students who desire to study additional subjects as well as those students who are required to repeat courses. Teachers will use the library during the summer months for study and research on curriculum problems.

Recruitment of librarians for the high school will become less difficult. Adequate staff in clearly defined positions will have removed the conditions that forced many librarians of the past to leave the school field. Some of our most able librarians have given up after several years during which their days were filled with never ending routine and housekeeping tasks, while important professional responsibilities like selection of materials had to be squeezed into evening hours at home. Position assignment by subject specialization will force professional librarians to attain competence in a subject area. The hopelessness many librarians formerly felt as they tried to keep abreast in all fields will be replaced by energy and zeal directed toward a clearly defined goal.

IMPLICATIONS OF NEW GOALS FOR LIBRARY QUARTERS

The library's responsibilities for acquiring, organizing, distributing, and housing the instructional materials and equipment of the school provide one important guide to planning physical quarters. Larger book collections and larger staffs are predicted, so both books and librarians will take up more space in the future library. How long and how frequently students use the library is a second element affecting the design of the library. The new educational goals stress the importance of individualized instruction and independent study. Obviously, how the school organizes its program to attain these goals affects the amount of space needed in the library.

The recent publication by the Commission on Experimental Study of the Utilization of the Staff in the Secondary Schools appointed by the National Association of Secondary-School Principals suggests abolishing the standard size class groups of 25–35 students meeting five days a week on inflexible schedules. It envisages three kinds of instruction: *large-group instruction* carried out in groups of 100 or more students, which will occupy about 40 per cent of the students' time; *small-group discussion* of from 12 to 15 students and the teacher, which will occupy about 20 per cent of the students' time; and *individual study,* which will occupy about 40 per cent of the students' time. In other words, the present thirty-hour school week will be divided so that students would spend eighteen hours in large and small groups and twelve hours in individual studies. During individual study periods, students would read, listen, view, question, experiment, examine, consider, analyze, investigate, think, write, create, memorize, record, make, visit, and self-appraise. The Commission suggests that these study activities will take place in project and material centers, museums, workshops, libraries, and laboratories, in and outside the school.[6] Since our new high-school library is a materials center, how many students will we need space for under such a revolutionary plan? If we estimate conservatively on the grounds that half the student study time would be spent outside the library, we shall need seating space for 20 per cent of the student body, or twice the present standards. (The college standard of seating space for one of every four students may be a safer estimate.) In this future high school, study halls as we know them will not exist. A variety of instructional and resource areas will replace the present series of standard classrooms, each designed to contain thirty students and one teacher. The library suite with its study-resource rooms will be an important area in the school and will require more space than the library in today's school.

I predict that the library in the future high school will be housed in multiple reading rooms. Each room will house materials in such broad subjects as social sciences, humanities, and sciences. In large schools additional rooms may be planned for more specific collections in art or music or technology. The maximum seating capacity for each reading room will probably be eighty; smaller rooms off each subject reading room will provide for another twenty to listen and view and confer individually or in small groups. This arrangement enables all forms of materials relevant to a broad subject area to be located in one division; librarians in charge will be subject specialists prepared to give expert assistance to teachers and students. Large schools may need central stack areas for lesser used books in each division. Separate rooms for the professional materials for teachers will be essential. Since

the one certain thing of the library's future is that book collections will grow and teaching methods change, library design must be flexible.

Although the extremely fluid organization suggested by the Commission referred to above may be adopted by only a few schools, I believe that all secondary schools will try to provide more intelligently for students' study time. I predict that the large study halls as we know them will be discarded and the space will be used for the library. The multiple-room library will be able to handle three or four classes who may need to use the library at the same time.

What about the library in the small high school? High schools of the size that educators deem necessary to offer a comprehensive education must have a library large enough to permit some specialization. Aside from duplication, a student body of three or four hundred will need as broad and varied a library collection as a student body of three or four thousand. The recent trend in larger schools toward division into "little schools," "houses," or small units will probably not alter our present pattern of concentration of the materials of the school in a central library. In the years to come, the high-school library will, in all likelihood, resemble a college library in size of collection, staff, and quarters.

DISTRICT AND REGIONAL MATERIALS CENTERS

There remains one other important aspect of the high-school library of the future which we must examine. In city school systems and in a growing number of consolidated school districts, the high-school library today is a part of a system-wide or district-wide organization of school libraries administered by a library supervisor or director. The

[6] *Ibid.,* pp. 7–14.

supervisor, among other duties, directs the work of a central staff who orders, catalogs, and processes materials for all libraries in the system. This centralization of acquisition and processing insures economy of time and effort and permits librarians in the school to use time and talent in work with teachers and students. Many of these school-library systems, in addition to centralized technical processing, provide model collections of books and materials to assist librarians in the individual schools in selection and bibliographical services such as special lists and a union catalog of all resources in the district.

Thoughtful school-library planners have realized for a number of years that the work of all school librarians will be immensely strengthened by an expansion of the bibliographical services of the central-school library systems. The concept of district materials centers was first noted in 1942 by Henne and Lowell, who conceived them to be "depositories under the direction of a staff of experts where all materials produced for children and high school students are housed and where those who are interested may come to examine the materials."[7] Under Henne's leadership and promotion the University of Chicago in 1945 established an instructional materials center. The work of the Children's Book Center as it is now known is probably familiar because of its monthly bulletin. Although it has never fulfilled all the requirements earlier suggested for a materials center, its discerning reviews of children's and young people's books and its service as an exhibit collection to librarians and teach-

ers within its geographical area are unique contributions. Bennett in 1943 included a materials center in her suggestions for a regional school-library system for Indiana.[8] Alice Brooks McGuire, the first librarian of the University of Chicago Children's Book Center, carried the idea further in a proposal in 1949 for a national system of materials centers which would serve the needs of both students and teachers in schools and colleges throughout the country. She suggested a system comprised of four main units: major regional centers in universities in New York City, Chicago, Texas, California, and Tennessee; smaller centers in metropolitan and county areas. The major centers would acquire, evaluate, and analyze the current output of *all* types of instructional materials and disseminate information about acceptable materials and would serve as research and experimental laboratories for the development, evaluation, analysis, and use of instructional materials. Smaller centers in teacher- and library-training institutions and in metropolitan or county areas would organize and administer a selective but adequate collection, keep the librarians and teachers informed about the work of the regional centers, and act as a laboratory for curriculum development and revision.[9]

In my crystal ball, I see one of the four regional centers in a university designated as the national center. A national system of materials centers will be better served by one rather than four "Libraries of Congress." Its acquisi-

[7] Frances Henne and Mildred Hawksworth Lowell, "Preparation of Secondary-School Teachers in the Use of Library Materials," *Library Quarterly,* XII (July, 1942), 556.

[8] Wilma Bennett, "A Plan for Regional Administration of School-Library Service in Indiana" (unpublished M.A. dissertation, Graduate Library School, University of Chicago, 1943), pp. 42–51.

[9] Alice R. Brooks, "The Role of Instructional Materials Centers in Schools and Colleges," *School Review,* LVII (October, 1949), 426–62.

tions department would acquire the current output of all instructional materials produced for students and teachers in printed and audio-visual forms. Its technical processes department would evaluate and analyze all materials and prepare critical annotations as well as cataloging and classifying all materials deemed worthy of recommendation. A research department would conduct research and experimentation in the analysis and use of materials and prepare special materials to fill unmet needs of schools. (This latter function may be handled by contract with authors outside the center.) A publications department would publish the critical reviews and catalog cards prepared by the technical processes division, while a circulation department would distribute materials produced by the center and those emanating from the network of regional, state, and local centers. A reference department would fill special bibliographical and information requests which could not be answered through the printed publications of the technical processes and research branch. Closed television and other forms of communication would accelerate reference and information service among the national, regional, and district centers.

These proposals, although visionary, have great relevance to the high-school library of the future. If smaller high schools outside city and consolidated district systems are to provide an education of high quality for their students, some method will have to be devised to strengthen the library resources and services in these schools. Librarians in smaller schools need processing and acquisition handled by central agencies; both librarians and teachers need the bibliographical services and help in book selection that their colleagues in cities are usually able to get from the central library. The work of all high-school librarians would be immeasurably improved if they could periodically examine a comprehensive collection of materials; if they could see critical reviews by competent specialists; and if they could buy printed cards analyzing theme, method, idea, and readability. It appears logical that materials centers in the future might be responsible for centralization of technical processing and acquisitions as well as for the maintenance of comprehensive exhibit collection and special bibliographical services. Many school-library systems provide such services now. In rural or small communities two or more school districts may establish a materials center on a co-operative basis.

SUMMARY

The secondary-school library of the future, like the secondary-school library of today, will not be able to give all the services requested of it. To paraphrase Sir Richard Livingston, "The good school library will be known by the number of useful things it declines to do." It will continue and strengthen those functions that relate directly to the selection, organization, interpretation, and use of materials. It will give first priority to serving teachers because only in this way can it truly serve all students. Increased demand for all kinds and forms of materials will require more library time for evaluation and selection. Teachers will require more analysis of materials than conventional subject catalogs and decimal classification now provide them. The library will continue to be responsible for reading guidance and library instruction, but its role will be primarily a consultant one in helping to plan and carry through the program in classes. This is not to say that the library will cease helping individual students but rather that both services will be more fully integrated with classroom work—they will grow out of it and lead back into it. The library will strengthen its services in selection, organization, and use of materials through dividing collections into broad subject areas and assigning to each librarians with special subject preparation. The library will furnish materials needed by teachers and counselors for personal and vocational guidance but will discontinue the student assistant organization and other direct guidance and counseling services. The library will co-operate with teachers in experimental use of materials with the handicapped as well as the able reader; the library will experiment with material organization and distribution. It will understand the desirability of district and regional centers and work toward their establishment.

A CRITICAL VIEW OF EDUCATIONAL MEDIA

ABRAM W. VANDER MEER

IT HAS become almost commonplace to say that change is the most distinctive characteristic of our time. We have been living in a world of rapid social, political, and technological change for about twenty-five years, and the next twenty-five or fifty years (if we survive) promise to bring even greater change. I am not sure whether I should say "promise" or "threaten" to bring change, for the frightening fact is that our very survival may well depend on our ability to react appropriately to change, perhaps to changes not yet even imagined.

A favorite motto in copybooks of a former generation was "knowledge is power." Our forebears wrote wiser than they knew. While they may have thought that the road to power through knowledge was open to all and that all knowledge was available for the seeking, they probably never visualized a time when, as now, knowledge gained in one's youth could not be expected to prepare one to meet the vicissitudes of life. This is a shrinking world but a vastly complex one. In order to survive we need to know our neighbor and be known by him. We need to know his goals and his means of achieving them.

All this has much to do with the importance of the topic on which I am to speak, that of educational media. Educational media are the means whereby knowledge is stored and transmitted and as one link in our chain of armor for survival, so to speak, they are as crucial as any of the other social, political, and military factors related to survival. Knowlege essential to this end must be made available to all people—old and young, the literate as well as the functionally illiterate.

Even if survival were not at issue, the violent changes in our own population place demands on educational media in at least three ways. The first derives from the huge increase in numbers of boys and girls of college age. The enormous increase in the absolute numbers of fourteen- to twenty-two-year-olds, to say nothing of the increasing percentage of college-age children who are seeking admission to colleges, will cause many institutions of higher learning, particularly the state supported, to increase enrolment from 50 to 100 per cent during the next decade. Second, at the precise time that the heaviest wave of students hits the colleges the hardest, the results of the so-called "baby famine" of the 1930's and early 1940's will be felt in the relative decrease in size of the group (young middle age) from which potential instructors and assistant professors are normally drawn. These two aspects of the population curve certainly presage many changes in the operation of our educational system. One change, certain to be brought about by having the maximum number of college students with the minimum number of men and women in their thirties to teach them, will be an increased reliance on educational media and on an educational system heavily dependent on individual

47

study. The transition from the present paternalistic "spoon-feeding" kind of education to reliance on independent study based on a variety of educational media will not be easy. It is sure to come, however, and to bring with it an important set of demands on educational media and on the people who manage them.

The third phenomenon of the population curve which places demands on educational media is an increased number of older people in our population. This year, for example, there are nearly 15½ million people in the United States over 65 years of age, a proportion of one out of eleven. In the next decade this is likely to increase to one out of nine or ten. These people, as well as their sons and daughters, must continue their education. As yet we know far too little about continuing education, but one thing of which we can be quite sure is that successful educational programs for adults and for older people demand a freedom of choice of content and, presumably, of media.

I could continue to list patterns of change which will have implications for educational media and for librarians and teachers who work with these media— for example, the increase in leisure time brought about by automation and the continual changes in kinds of skills and abilities required to earn a living—but it is not my purpose here to do more than indicate an awareness of the tremendous importance of educational media. Because they grow out of the society in which we live and the needs and goals that are related both to survival and to human happiness, they merit critical consideration.

So that this view may not be altogether negative, I shall, after listing five or six areas where improvement is ob-

viously needed, present an equal number of hopeful signs. Shortcomings and hopeful signs are derived from and relate to the media themselves and to the people who are interested in and working in their production, distribution, and use.

It seems to me that the most noticeable shortcoming of educational media today is the preoccupation with almost anything rather than content. Regardless of the type of medium one studies, one must conclude that most of them are dominated by the motive of *something to sell* rather than *something to say*. We have, for example, our booklists of "best sellers." Perhaps the worth of some books may be gauged by the number of copies sold, but this is surely a highly fallible rule. In television and radio, too, there is the same type of preoccupation. The measure of the worth of a program is, at least in the eyes of the sponsors, the size of the mass audience, whether measured in terms of percentage of sets tuned to a particular program or in terms equally well designed to provide a convenient, sizable statistic. The British, on the other hand, have been quite proud of their "Third Program" although its audience has often fallen below 100,000. But it is only since television came on the scene that radio has begun to concern itself with the kinds of communication which should have occupied it before, such as foreign-language broadcasting, more adequate news coverage, and better special features which, before TV, were not sufficiently profitable to engage the interest of radio. For further evidence of the neglect of content, consider the audiovisual field. Here we have advocates of the filmstrip, the motion picture, opaque projection, slides, etc., to name some of the competing camps. If a filmstrip series is "successful," before long there will be a motion-picture series on the same subject, or vice versa. Neither a filmstrip nor a motion picture is often made with the main thought of presenting ideas and concepts best suited to the particular medium. Of course, we now have an even larger competing group producing television.

The second major criticism of educational media is the lack of availability *to individuals* of the means of communication. Anyone can write a book, to be sure, but let him try to get it published. Of course, all the major publishers bring out "prestige" books, but the young author has a hard struggle to find a publisher. Too often the odds are too great and the fight is given up before a publisher is found. Yet the printed word is by all odds the most readily available means of communication for the individual. To express one's self and one's ideas by broadcast or film is an extensive operation—a team operation. In the absence of a sizable amount of investment capital these media are largely unavailable to individuals. The motion picture still costs at least a thousand dollars per minute to produce and put on the market, radio time is costly, and a video tape recorder that can be bought for under ten thousand dollars is only beginning to appear. If, as we believe, the strength of a democracy is in the genius of its people as individuals, there ought to be some way whereby individuals, largely on their own initiative, can readily communicate their ideas to a mass audience.

A third major criticism of educational media is that they seem to be dominated by the concept of learning as "pouring in" rather than as stimulating self-activity. A friend of mine once made a point by saying that the word *education* came

from the Greek and was a form of the verb *educare*, which means *to lead out*. Not so, said a detractor, it comes from the DuPont Company of Wilmington, Delaware; that is, from the word Duco, which is a kind of polish. Whichever meaning one prefers, too many modern examples of educational media fail to conform. Textbooks in the classic sense —that is, books of texts which are to be thought about, elaborated, developed, weighed, evaluated—are a rarity. The average textbook today, whether for the third grade or the college senior, is much more likely to be a complete printed course, decorated with many pictures, illustrations, and other eye-catchers. An excellent case in point is a recent audiovisual textbook, by Brown, Lewis, and Harcleroad.[1] This is an excellent book, but no more a *textbook* than Fanny Farmer's cookbook is. The fact is, that the book in question is probably the very best compendium of good practice and how-to-do-it information likely to become available in the audio-visual field for the next decade. The trouble is, however, that it provides a wealth of vicarious experience without really getting down to the principles that motivate or explain such experience. In a changing world a body of basic theoretical principles is the most practical thing that anyone can have. Nearly all modern educational media are short on principles and long on the communication of day-to-day experience.

Here I should like to recommend an interesting exercise to librarians. Measure the number of inches of shelf space required by fifty textbooks published between 1920 and 1925, and then meas-

[1] James W. Brown, Richard B. Lewis, and Fred F. Harcleroad, *A-V Instruction: Materials and Methods* (New York: McGraw-Hill Book Co., 1959).

ure the shelf space required for the same number published between 1950 and 1955. The increase in size of the textbook can hardly be explained solely by the incorporation of more information. It is due partially to the preference for communicating unstructured experience rather than texts and principles; and partially to our preoccupation with "eye appeal." The austere textbook is the exception rather than the rule. The excessive interest in eye appeal is particularly noticeable in the television spectacular. The simple story, simply told, is almost never anything more than a starting point. When a simple program gains an audience, it usually also gains a high-powered production crew to elaborate it. In a very real sense, too, the motion-picture industry, particularly when directed toward informational films, suffers from the same defect. More than ten years ago Charles Hoban demonstrated what is known as the "cameo" technique for teaching-films. This technique eliminated sets, settings, and background and concentrated on showing only the absolutely essential on the screen. I had the pleasure of experimentally validating the technique and followed the experiment with several more —all of which led to the same conclusion: namely, that such techniques as the dramatized story line, background music, special effects, etc., had little or nothing to add to the teaching power of the film. On the positive side, too, the Instructional Film Research Program of the Pennsylvania State University has produced several highly successful training films utilizing their so-called "minimum production technique." All this research has made interesting reading for students who write term papers, but the motion-picture producer is not reading it, and (to judge from his prod-

uct) when he does read, he does not believe it.

The persistence of separatism is a fourth critical shortcoming in educational media. This shortcoming refers to the people who work with the media. There appear to be four sizable and relatively distinct groups, each too much unaware, or, worse, too suspicious, of the other three. The four groups are librarians, audio-visual people, radio and television people, and the "communication experts" in the fields of speech and semantics. There are more elements in common among these four groups than there are distinguishing differences. The trouble is that this very elementary and obvious fact is overlooked by so many people. One hopeful sign exists in this complex, and I will speak about it in a moment.

Philosophic differences among the groups stem in part from apparently different conceptions of how learning takes place. It is incontrovertible that films and broadcasts tend toward "imposed" learning, while books tend toward "self-directed learning." The fact is, of course, that films and broadcasts need *not* be made to foster imposed learning; and thirty million school children can furnish examples of books used to *impose* learning on unwilling scholars.

The final shortcoming that I wish to point out concerning educational media relates to a lack of general understanding of the total process of communication and the related fact that the medium is only one part—albeit a crucial part—of that process. The communication process has been described as consisting of units of "who says what to whom, under what conditions, and with what effect." Too many producers and users of educational media—librarians and teachers alike—take an extremely ethnocentric view of the "to whom" part; that is the recipient of the communication process. Here is an example: I recently had occasion to read the report of a research study which purported to test the effect of homogeneous grouping on learning by television. The homogeneity present in this particular research came from grouping together the students in the upper third of their large class when tested on the material presented during the first few weeks of the course. Half of these so-called "superior students" were pulled out of the large television class and given a separate room to themselves. The remainder stayed with their presumably average fellows.

Now it seems to me quite possible that the students who received high marks on the first test got them partly as a function of their aptitude, but it seems at least plausible that an additional factor was at work, namely, what Dr. Herbert Thelen of the University of Chicago terms "life style." I would hypothesize that the personality of some people is well adapted to learning in the highly structured situation normally presented by television and as it was presented by television in the class in which this research was conducted. The so-called "life style" of other people, however, may be such as to find such a highly structured learning system quite frustrating and perhaps a barrier to their most effective learning. When I protested to this particular researcher that he had not availed himself of the opportunity at least to test the hypothesis that achievement in a particular kind of class situation might be related to some factors other than aptitude, method of teaching being held constant, he was quite indignant and displayed very little interest in discussing the matter even as

a hypothetical possibility. It is this lack of appreciation of the various characteristics of learners as they may be related to the effectiveness of different kinds of educational media that account, in my opinion, for many of the discouraging research results summed up in the often repeated phrase "no significant differences."

Television, of course, and television teaching, is not alone in its lack of understanding of the recipient of communications. Some of us remember that famous cartoonist, Webster, who had a whole series of humorous incidents based on this theme and entitled "The Unseen Audience." There is an unseen and often largely ignored audience for books as well as for any other medium. Why do most writers of children's books, particularly in the basic reading series, insist on uniformly portraying the family as upper middle class, white suburbanites? The mother of Dick and Jane is always at home to play with the children, bake cookies, or tend the house. She never combines motherhood with school teaching, librarianship, or factory work. Dick and Jane's father seems always to be another man in a gray flannel suit. He always carries a brief case rather than a lunch bucket, he never works the night shift, and he is the dominant figure in the household. Not only is this a myth, but it is also a handicap for a sizable minority of readers.

There are many other examples of the lack of knowledge of the total communication process and lack of the application of such knowledge on the part of the producers and users of educational media; an example is the general failure to make the distinction between media and channels, which explains much of the meaningless controversy between advocates of television instruction and its opponents. Another example is the almost total preoccupation with media and channels rather than with the learning environment in which the media and channels are used, and with the general method of instruction rather than with the organization of experience in such a way as to produce the most permanent learning for the most people.

In spite of the weaknesses discussed here, there are hopeful signs and developments. It will not surprise you, I am sure, if these hopeful signs and developments parallel rather closely the shortcomings previously mentioned. It is, I think, a legitimate function of criticism to point out shortcomings, but it is also the obligation of the critic to indicate where progress is being made.

If, as I have said, the educational media are not completely available to all the individuals whose ideas merit availability, it would be hard to convince a foreign visitor of this fact. Librarians keep needing additions to the library to house new books and materials; cumulative book indexes require more shelf space each year, as does the H. W. Wilson *Guide to Educational Films*. The Sunday edition of the *New York Times* has enough in it to keep the average person in reading matter from one Sunday to the next. A dozen television channels grind out programs day and night, as do the hundreds of radio stations. Speaking of the volume of broadcasts, John Crosby once said: "The best of it is wonderful and the worst of it is terrible; the trouble is, the worst outnumbers the best by a hundred to one." If we are starving for educational media, we are indeed starving in the midst of plenty. The fact is, of course, that winnowing the good from the indifferent is a real challenge, a task which for some people may require the assistance of librarians

and other workers in the educational media field. Vigorous and forward-looking programs of education for these specialists are increasing in number, and professionally prepared people are being graduated in greater numbers than ever before.

Earlier in this paper I referred to the separatism among four groups of people working with educational media. I think one hopeful sign in this connection is that we are well on our way to real *rapprochement* between the audio-visualists and the librarians. As an example, I cite the fact that the 1960 edition of the *Evaluative Criteria* published by the Co-operative Study of Secondary School Standards will include a section which lists criteria relating to the entire range of educational media. No little credit for this fine achievement, in which the important concerns of librarians and audio-visual directors are merged without any loss of identity for either group, goes to Walter Stone and Alice Lohrer of the University of Illinois. In the *Evaluative Criteria* it is recognized that trained personnel with adequate resources in the educational media field are essential to secondary schools. Whether these resources are administered by the librarian or by the audio-visual educator, or by some individual whose training and competence reflects both, is less important than the fact that the facilities are used. Meanwhile, however, the instructional materials center rarely includes radio or television. This is the challenge that must be given number one priority in this particular area.

A third hopeful sign is the broadening of scholarship concerning educational media. More and more the training received by librarians includes basic work in the newer educational media and, equally important, in serious study of the historical, philosophical, and psychological bases of education and communication. By the same token the training of teachers and audio-visual education people is slowly beginning to incorporate basic training in librarianship.

A fourth hopeful sign, closely related to that of broadened scholarship, is the dramatic upsurge in research in educational media. If my understanding of the situation is correct, the Educational Media Branch of the United States Office of Education was able, during the fiscal year 1958–59, to distribute $1,600,000 for the support of research in these media under the National Defense Education Act. The fact that this Act exists and that it includes a section on research in media of communication is a most exciting and hopeful sign. I understand that more than 335 applications for research grants were received and acted upon by June 30, 1959. Most of these proposals came from colleges and universities rather than from school systems and libraries. The preoccupation in these applications with television and kinescope recording to the neglect of other media of instruction must be considered unfortunate; however, this too can and undoubtedly will change. Additional impressions of the studies of the National Defense Education Act under the Newer Educational Media branch are that the research is more general than analytical, more applied than basic, and too much at the college level to the exclusion of adult education and precollege education. However, the faith and support that the Congress of the United States has placed in all of us who work with educational media is, to me, one of the most heartening signs of our times.

One series of experiments constitutes, I believe, a development of sufficient importance to merit particular mention as a "hopeful sign," namely, the whole idea of programming of information and media which is being opened up by B. F. Skinner and his associates. Perhaps the greatest limiting factor of educational films, recordings, and the like has been that they have not been truly under the control of the learner. In the past, the learner has had to invest too much time simply in finding out whether a film or recording suited his needs. Skinner and his teaching machine will show us whether this must continue to be the case. As I understand it, the teaching machine permits the programming of a variety of teaching materials and devices based on individual patterns of need as derived from the responses of the learner.

Engraved above the entrance of the library at my university, Pennsylvania State, are the words "The true university is a collection of books." I do not know how many of the hundreds of students who daily pass under the motto even notice it, or, of those who do, how many are impressed. I feel sure, however, that if we interpret the word *book* to stand as a type for all media that store and transmit knowledge, the motto is truer today than it has ever been.

THE ROLE OF THE FEDERAL GOVERNMENT
IN SCHOOL-LIBRARY DEVELOPMENT

MARY HELEN MAHAR

Two recent federal laws, the Library Services Act of 1956 and the National Defense Education Act of 1959, have profoundly affected school libraries, although neither law mentions them. The purpose of the Library Services Act is "to promote the further development of public library service in rural areas."[1] In 1957 the American Association of School Librarians, a division of the American Library Association, issued a statement indorsed by the board of directors of the Public Libraries Division of ALA which says, in part: "It [the Board of Directors of the American Association of School Librarians] believes that if funds provided by this Act [the Library Services Act] were used to finance a library within a school, such use would be contrary to the intent of this legislation and would deter the development of school libraries within schools."

The National Defense Education Act aims "to strengthen the National defense and to encourage and assist in the expansion and improvement of educational programs to meet critical National needs; and for other purposes."[2]

Both laws are administered by the United States Office of Education and by official state agencies. Within the Office of Education the Library Services Act is administered by special staff of the Library Services Branch; the National Defense Education Act is administered by several branches of the Office but not the Library Services Branch. No responsibility for either law is assigned to the Specialist for School and Children's Libraries. I am, therefore, in the peculiar position of interpreting two laws which are silent on the subject of school libraries and whose administration is none of my official business. I have had, however, considerable opportunity to observe and participate in discussions on the Library Services Act and the National Defense Education Act as they affect school libraries, and so it is as a practiced deducer of inferences that I have the temerity to present this paper.

We have known for a long time that great inequities exist in educational services over the country. Support of public schools and libraries has been determined often by the ability of the local community to raise taxes for education. Children and youth in communities with a high per capita income usually have superior schools and libraries, and those in less fortunate, or very sparsely settled areas, have substandard schools and libraries. Some states through various plans of financial aid have effected a more even distribution of state funds for education; nevertheless, the geographic location of millions of boys and girls in the United States still determines the quality of public educational institutions available to them. Many other factors, of course, have influence on the quality of educa-

[1] Public Law 597 (84th Cong.), H.R. 2840.

[2] Public Law 85-864 (85th Cong.), H.R. 13247.

tion—community attitudes toward education, tax structure, and population mobility, among them. However, rural areas generally need financial help to develop good schools and public libraries.

The Library Services Act is intended "to promote the further extension by the several States of public library services to rural areas without such services, or with inadequate services." State programs of public library service under the Library Services Act have made wide use of the bookmobile, which stops at local libraries, branches, and community centers. Often the sole rural community center is the school, which the bookmobile reaches every two weeks or so. Since public libraries serve the whole community, including children, and since rural children are most readily accessible in schools, it is inevitable that the development of rural public library service, espcially bookmobile service, would lead to schoolhouse doors. Furthermore, the rural have-nots of public libraries are also have-nots of school libraries. A major concern of county and regional public librarians developing library service under the Library Services Act has been that service to rural children while in school has absorbed an undue proportion of public library funds and staff time at the expense of library service to the whole community. Many public librarians share the misgivings of school librarians that bookmobile stops at rural schools will deter the development of school libraries administered by boards of education. Supplementary service to school libraries is an accepted and needed function of public libraries. Public library service as a substitute for school libraries has long been regarded by the library profession as at best a temporary expedient, in both rural and urban communities.

The Library Services Act has provided a new impetus to school librarians and public librarians to re-examine their basic philosophies of service, to define for boards of education and library boards their respective functions, and to interpret to community members the separate and complementary functions of school libraries and public libraries. These three tasks are difficult; there are no hard-and-fast rules which can be applied in every state, region, or county, and they require sound think-

TABLE 1*

State	Total No. of Schools	Total No. of One-Teacher Schools
A.............	4,911	3,431
B.............	3,355	2,638
C.............	2,847	2,221
D.............	1,239	820

* Source: *Biennial Survey of Education in the United States, 1954–56* (Washington, D.C.: U.S. Department of Health, Education, and Welfare, 1959), chap. ii: "Statistics of State School Systems, 1955–56," pp. 42–43.

ing by professional leaders. In some states professional librarians have shown qualities of leadership in attacking these problems, and both school and public librarians have worked with acumen toward their solution. For example, as a direct result of the stimulus of the Library Services Act, in three states public and school librarians are working for the appointment of state school-library supervisors. In other states, however, the lack of professional leadership and perhaps a lack of understanding of the need for professional leadership are real detriments to the development of school libraries.

Let us take a look at the number of one-teacher schools in four States as compared with the total number of schools (Table 1). School libraries do not usually exist in one-teacher schools, of which there are still 34,964 among 130,473 elementary and secondary schools in the United States. The reduction of the number of one-teacher schools in the last twenty-five years is an index of a vast program of school-district consolidation. In 1931–32 there were 143,391 one-teacher schools as compared with the present number of 34,964. Further consolidation is, of course, possible, but, if rural children are going to live at home while they attend school, some very small schools will remain part of the national educational pattern.

In the public library field, the Library Services Act has stimulated the creation of county and regional systems which serve small library centers within the systems. The further development of intermediate units of school administration should open the way for new and improved school-library service from county or regional boards of education. This type of service, already existing in rural areas, can provide basic school-library collections in every small school and professional school librarians whose time can be apportioned among several small schools of an administrative unit. If these intermediate units employ curriculum specialists as well as school librarians, the in-service training of teachers in the building of curriculum and the use of materials would help to produce small schools of quality. The Library Services Act has focused attention on the needs of rural schools in library service. The National Defense Education Act and other forces operating in education at this time have many possibilities to assist substantially in the improvement of not only rural but urban and suburban school libraries.

The implications of the National De-fense Education Act for school libraries, especially in relation to certain areas of curriculum, are direct and far-reaching. A law "to encourage and assist in the expansion and improvement of educational programs" includes school libraries as essential services to elementary and secondary education. The National Defense Education Act is a complicated law; it affects elementary and secondary public and non-public schools, colleges and universities, educational research, the dissemination of educational information, and the professional preparation of school, college, and university personnel. Whenever a new program of education at any level is developed, it is axiomatic that new and extended collections of materials must be provided, and libraries are the acknowledged method for the organization and circulation of materials in educational institutions.

Because libraries are service agencies, however, to the whole school program and the entire school community, they are likely to be accepted as a matter of fact, and, because often the professional preparation of teachers has not included the school library as an educational method, the needs of school libraries as agencies essential to vital educational programs are not recognized. Nevertheless, school-library materials and services cannot be dissociated from school programs. Two titles of the National Defense Education Act illustrate this point. Title III, "Financial Assistance for Strengthening Science, Mathematics and Modern Foreign Language Instruction," specifically provides funds for printed materials (other than textbooks) and audio-visual materials. Title V, "Guidance, Counseling and Testing, Identification and Encouragement of Able Students," makes no mention of materials; nevertheless, in the interpretation of this title, funds may be used for materials.

Several interpretations of the National Defense Education Act in relation to libraries have appeared in print: *Library Opportunities in the National Defense Education Act,* prepared by the American Library Association, and the "National Defense Education Act, School Librarians and School Libraries," which appeared in the *Wilson Library Bulletin,* in June, 1959, and available as a reprint from the Library Service Branch of the Office of Education. In this paper the discussion will attempt to go beyond these interpretations and discuss ways in which school libraries and librarians are intrinsic to the purposes of the National Defense Education Act.

Let us note the language of Title III, "Financial Assistance for Strengthening Science, Mathematics, and Modern Foreign Language Instruction." This title provides for state plans setting forth the improvement of instruction by the acquisition of materials, and equipment, by minor remodeling of buildings to accommodate new materials and equipment, and by the expansion or improvement of state supervisory or related services in public elementary and secondary schools; in brief, the improvement of instruction through materials, equipment, quarters, and supervision. A principal of a small high school looks at this title, at his state plan for employing federal funds under it, and then at his school's science program. He has one course in general science, one in biology, and one in physics, taught alternating years with chemistry. Every student is required to take general science or biology; the other sciences may be elected. He looks at his science classrooms and laboratories— too small classrooms, inadequately equipped laboratories, no facilities for the demonstration of science techniques. He looks at his school library— perhaps a few standard texts in each science field, five or six biographies of scientists, some science fiction, four or five filmstrips on nature study, two science periodicals. He looks at his community—a small one of 2,500 people, anxious to have a good high school; at his students, some of them very able, eager to learn, all of them are worthy of the best in education, and capable of contributing to society. This principal wants to submit a project for the improvement of science instruction under the National Defense Education Act to his state education department.

To whom does he turn? He calls together his science teachers, his guidance director, and his librarian. He knows this group well—their strengths and weaknesses. Planning new science courses, learning more about pupils' aptitudes, constructing lists of books, periodicals, pamphlets, filmstrips, films, tapes, and recordings to fit the pupils' needs in the science programs, planning for their use, determining kinds of equipment to purchase, and expansion of space—these are the difficult and interrelated tasks of this group. The principal must lead his group to plan together, each contributing his special knowledge to the various aspects of this project but each taking part in the whole plan.

This principal sees that his planning committee needs some help. His teachers are not sure how to construct an advanced physics course; and his librarian needs more background on sources of science materials; his whole group needs stimulation in understanding newer concepts of science instruction, including the use of many materials, in secondary schools. This school is, fortunately, located in a state where the plan for Title III provides for additional state supervisory and consultative personnel in science instruction and in school-library materials. These supervisors on request come together to his school and work as consultants with the committee in developing a project which will provide superior science instruction designed for the students of this high school. The school library will support this course of study with up-to-date titles in general science, biology, physics, chemistry, with books on the relationship of science to the welfare of society, with thoughtful and inspiring biographies of great scientists, with demonstration filmstrips, a substantial number of scientific periodicals, and professional materials for the science teachers.

This school's work on a project under Title III is an example of strengthening instruction, of which the school library is an integral part. It is possible that school-library materials may be the only weak aspect in a school's instructional program; nevertheless, an approach which includes all the elements of instruction will better fulfil the intent of Title III, and the general purposes of education for which effective school-library service is so essential. This basic principle may apply to the strengthening of instruction in mathematics and modern foreign languages, in individual, elementary and secondary schools, and in school systems, and, under Titte VIII, in Area Vocational Education Programs. In support of guidance programs under Title V, as well, secondary-school administrators, guidance directors, teach-

ers, and librarians should study the whole guidance program and its needs and relate library materials to the school's project for the establishment and maintenance of programs of testing, guidance, and counseling. It should be noted here, however, that the state plans for Titles III, V, and VIII are the final determinants of methods for developing school projects, and it is important for educators in states to know and study their own state plans.

The National Defense Education Act has brought into sharper focus some of the very fundamental needs of school librarians and school libraries. Let us look again at the librarian in the school just described where she may be working on the improvement of instruction not only in science, but in mathematics, modern foreign languages, and, indeed, all the elements of the school's curriculum. The school librarian in this small school is expected to know the psychology of children and young people, the young people of this particular high school, philosophy of education, curriculum, instruction, materials, and library organization and administration. She is also expected to be a mature individual with insight and sympathy, able to work effectively with her principal, teachers, and pupils. The intellectual dsciplines of school librarianship have great depth, and, although this fact has been recognized by leaders in the field, in practice, the professional preparation of school librarians has not achieved anything near the substance it requires.

We must look in two directions for the answer to this state of affairs; the school librarian shares the undernourished state of the teaching profession and occupies an uncertain position in the library profession. In attempting to overcome the teacher shortage, requirements in the preparation of teachers, including school librarians, have been cut back, or held down; other measures to overcome this shortage have been tried, such as the selection of a relatively few master teachers to teach by television and the use of teacher-helpers. These emergency or experimental methods have not improved so far the school librarian's opportunity to contribute to instruction. The problem of the teacher shortage has yet to be generally attacked at its roots by setting high standards for teachers (including school librarians), extending professional preparation to five or six years, and raising salaries. In the library profession recognition has come slowly to its youngest members, the school librarians, and there has been very slow growth of understanding that elementary and secondary education is just as demanding a discipline for librarians as higher education, adult education, law, medicine, or the various branches of technology. State departments of education, in struggling with shortages of school librarians, and lack of financial support for schools, tend in some cases to accept minimum standards in the professional preparation of school librarians as the optimum in goals. *Certification of School Librarians,* the study completed last year in the Office of Education, contains evidence of this fact.

There have been only sporadic and isolated attempts to relate the professional education of school librarians and teachers. In addition to the broad background the school librarian should bring to her job, she needs often to conduct an in-service program for teachers on school library materials and their use. School librarians have been very vocal about the magnitude of their work. The literature of librarianship is full of articles on the purpose and problems of school-library service. One of the unfortunate outcomes of these interpretations has been that school librarians are often regarded as too self-assertive, repetitious, and self-pitying, because they think themselves misunderstood. The truth is that they are misunderstood.

It is surely time for those concerned with the professional education of school librarians and teachers—directors of library and teacher education, state departments of educations, school administrators, and school library and curriculum personnel to examine the function of school librarianship and to define its true professionalism. Perhaps a national conference to encourage reflection and initiate study of these questions would be a good beginning. Their clarification for both the teaching and the library professions would be of tremendous value to American schools and libraries.

Titles II and IV of the National Defense Education Act have important potentialities for school librarianship. Title II establishes student loan funds, administered by participating institutions of higher education, for "students with a superior acdemic background who express a desire to teach in elementary and secondary schools." The interpretation of Title II includes students who may wish to become school librarians and permits the use of the loans by undergraduate or graduate students. Title IV provides for fellowships in new or expanded graduate programs "to further the objective of increasing facilities available in the Nation for the graduate training of college or university level teachers." These new or expanded programs may be in any field, and the graduate schools of librarianship could qualify with a program for librarians interested in preparing for continuing study in library education. These two titles can help not only in the education of school librarians for individual schools but also in the professional preparation and doctoral study of teachers of library education. We cannot hope to strengthen school librarianship, or any type of librarianship, unless we give attention to the needs of teachers and leaders in library education. Title VII, "Research and Experimentation in More Effective Utilization of Television, Radio, Motion Pictures, and Related Media for Educational Purposes," has, I believe, implications for library education in the training of school librarians for the utilization of such media and in using the new media in library education. Library schools and divisions of library education should study this title as a possible means of support for research and experimentation in developing new methods and materials for these two areas.

The federal government has shown great interest in educational research, through the National Defence Education Act recently established, the Cooperative Research Program, which administers federal grants to universities and state departments of education, and, of course, in its time-honored support of the Office of Education program of educational research and statistics. There are, indeed, many implications for research in relation to school libraries: we need research concerning them as they affect our children and youth, and we need to encourage school libraries to include books and materials for teachers concerning educational research.

The Library Services Branch of the Office of Education is a part of the Division of Research and Statistics. This division also includes the Educatonal Media Branch, which administers Title VII of the National Defense Education Act, the Cooperative Research Branch, and the Educational Statistics Branch. Title VII also provides for grants or contracts "to foster research and experimentation in the development and evaluation of projects involving television, radio, motion pictures and related media of communication which may prove of value to State or local educational agencies in the operation of their public elementary and secondary schools." The school library includes newer media, and its function in the organization and effective use of all materials is surely a valid and needed subject for research. The Cooperative Research Program is currently sponsoring the study at Rutgers University Graduate School of Library Service, "Effectiveness of the Elementary-School Library," which will have great significance for elementary education. There are many other possibilities for cooperative research studies in the library field—a much-needed study is that of school and public library relationships.

The Library Services Branch continues its program of statistical and research studies in libraries. One of the new contributions of the Branch will be its forthcoming periodic publication, *Library Research in Progress,* which will centralize information on research concerning all types of libraries and should stimulate new ideas for investigaton.

A very important implication for school libraries is the role of the federal government in encouraging the development of supervision. Title III includes financial aid for the employment of state supervisors of public elementary and secondary schools in the fields of science, mathematics, and modern foreign languages and for the administration of the state plan. Depending upon the state plans for Title III, the supervision of school libraries, through the "related services" provision of Title III, may be supported by funds under this title. School librarians should study state plans in order to ascertain how school-library supervisors in state education agencies could fit into these programs and inform administrators of the possibilities for the improvement of instruction through the extension and development of school-library supervision.

Over the years the Office of Education has held conferences of school-library supervisors for the exchange of ideas and the discovery of new methods to encourage growth in school-library service. The Office frequently holds conferences of supervisors in other fields of instruction. Concepts of school-library supervision have changed from direction and control of school libraries to guidance and stimulation of the professional growth of school librarians and to partnership in the consultative activities of other supervisory specialists working with schools. Supervision of school libraries is at a new stage of growth, not only in the spread of modern concepts, but in the extension of supervisory services to all the states and to many more communities. The first great impetus to state school-library supervision was provided in the early 1930's by the General Education Board with salaries for supervisors in several Southern States. The responsibility for the salaries of these supervisors was taken over by the states, and, in every case, these positions have continued in state departments of education. The support of supervision in

the National Defense Education Act is fresh evidence of recognition not only of the importance of supervision and the need for its development but also of its requirements in financial support.

For some years prior to the creation of the Library Services Division, the Office of Education employed a school libraries specialist, and, since the inception of the Division in 1936, there has been a specalist for school and children's libraries in continual service. Research, the collection of statistics, professional publications, and consultative services to the field in school and children's libraries continue to be the basic functions of this position. It provides unique opportunities for co-operative efforts with specialists in school administration and elementary, secondary, vocational, and international education of the Office of Education. For example, the publication *School Library Materials in Science, Mathematics, Modern Languages and Guidance and How To Use Them* was prepared in the Library Services Branch to assist school librarians and teachers in the location, selection, and use of materials in these fields; it represents the combined suggestions of many Office of Education specialists and research for additional materials by staff of the Library Services Branch.

At the request of the Study Commission of Chief State School Officers, we are conducting presently in the Library Services Branch a study on "State Department of Education Responsibilities and Services for School Libraries," and we hope to complete the report of this study for publication during the coming school year of 1959–60. We are also initiating an annual post-card statistical survey of school libraries to provide basic data on school libraries in between the comprehensive survey which has been published every six years as a chapter in the *Biennial Survey of Education.*

The Office of Education is expanding in size and in scope through the administration of federal legislation in education, broadened research, and a heightened program in publications and consultation. Nevertheless, it remains a service agency to both institutions and individuals seeking its assistance. Federal aid to education is in itself a service, available to agencies and individuals when they request it.

In school-library development the federal government has made available assistance in the strengthening of school libraries, the professional education of school librarians, the supervision of school libraries, and research concerned with school libraries. These are broad areas with which the school-library profession is concerned in bringing about the quality of school-library service to education in which we all believe. School librarians and libraries have always contributed to the fundamental purpose of schools—the education of individuals in a free society. The 1960 White House Conference on Children and Youth provides an exceptional opportunity for school librarians to interpret the potentialities and goals of school libraries in serving education.

SCHOOL AND PUBLIC LIBRARY RELATIONSHIPS

SARA INNIS FENWICK

THE broad aspects of school and public library relationships have been well treated during the last ten years in our professional literature —by Mildred Batchelder in her historical summary in *Library Trends,* January, 1953; by Frances Henne and Frances L. Spain in *Annals of the American Academy of Political and Social Science,* November, 1955; and, recently, in the February, 1959, issue of the ALA *Bulletin* by Lowell Martin, Mary Helen Mahar, and others. It would be of little value for me to try to repeat the thoughtful analyses of the problem which have been made so ably by these authors. On the other hand, it would not seem that the school library could be properly examined in its various aspects without recognizing the importance of school and public library relationships, if only from one angle— that of total library resources for children and young people in a community. For however poor the communication is between the two types of libraries in any given community, there is one point at which they meet, and that is in the experience of the young people themselves with library resources. The school librarian may never set foot inside the public library, and the public librarian may never visit the school, but at least one-third of the youth in the community know and use the resources and services of both, if they are reasonably good libraries, the proportion of school-age youth who are borrowers of the public library is from a half to two-thirds.

Let us suppose that we have the community of professional daydreams where there are good library facilities in both school and public library. Consider then the experience of the average young person as he grows through childhood and adolescence. This youth has been accustomed to using libraries since he could hold a book in his hands. His parents took him to the public library; they brought books home to read to him; they gave him a chance to choose his own books and to have a library card of his own as soon as he asked for it and knew what it represented. He was taken to preschool story hours at the public library and learned to enjoy stories and books with other children of his own age. He discovered that this building which his parents seemed to consider an important and pleasant place to go also had a special spot and a program planned just for him. He found out that reading was a rewarding activity and that libraries had answers to many questions, that the range of subjects in books was as wide as his interests, and that the librarians would give him the guidance and help he needed.

When he went to school, he found a library meeting the same needs. As a kindergarten pupil he found all his favorite picture and story books and enjoyed hearing stories told in the library. He was eager to read, and, as his skill increased, he found that he needed more and more books. As the years went by in elementary school, his interests widened. He read all the books in the school library that interested

63

him, and he was fortunate to find that in many areas of his special interests, when he had exhausted the school-library collection, there were more books on the subject, or by his favorite author, in the public library; and, furthermore, the librarian would see that he had access to every book that he needed, whether it was in her department or not. The browsing he could do in the broader collection of the public library, selected as it was to provide an open door to knowledge to all members of the community, would open new doors to him too. Skills in using books, films, filmstrips, recordings, tapes, as tools to solve problems and to locate information were learned in school classes and in the school library and transferred to the use of the collection in the public library, so that, when this youth graduated, he knew that there were resources in his community whereby he could continue his education, formally or informally, all his life.

This is the way a young person has grown up in one of our urban centers where school and public library facilities have been well developed. There was always a professionally trained librarian to guide him—a librarian who knew books and understood what he needed. Both librarians, school and public, had a single goal as far as he was concerned: to make reading an ever rich source of experience and to help him become an intelligent user of all sources of communication.

There were differences in the book collection, chiefly differences of focus. The school collection was developed to provide resources for a rich curriculum oriented to all the needs and interests of the youth of the community. The public library collection represented the interests, concerns, and needs of the entire community and its age range from cradle to old age. There were more books on more subjects, more specialized reference books, more periodicals; especially there were books to grow into as he broadened his interests. The school librarian was more likely to know the materials he needed for classroom research. She worked with his teachers; she knew his parents; she had helped him learn to read and to find his way among the books and within them. She had seen his plays, admired and displayed his artwork, and exhibited his classroom productions. He had probably worked as an assistant to her. But the public librarian was also a very good friend of his. She could help him to use all the books in the entire library to answer his questions. She seemed to understand better than he did the special kind of book he needed at a particular time. He remembered the long talks he had had with her about the books they had enjoyed together. This young person was fortunate to have had books in abundance wherever he needed them in the community.

Not all young people grow up in this kind of community, unfortunately. We know from our own experience as well as from reports and surveys of the field how great is the range of library services. In considering the experience and the need of a young person, whatever community he lives in, we need to look critically at the total availability and accessibility of materials, printed and otherwise. There is a total need here, in the realization and satisfaction of which two agencies, school and public library, are involved.

In the course of his education every young person needs a really vast amount of learning materials of all kinds. In the evolving school of tomorrow the large blocks of time which the student spends in individual research will not be rewarding unless there be a rich environment of materials and guides to stimulate further search when his interest is aroused and to encourage a desire to pursue knowledge that will keep him searching all his life.

With these needs of youth in mind, I found it challenging to examine the total library resources available to young people of high-school age in a very limited region of twenty-seven Chicago suburban communities. It was impossible to make comparisons at the elementary level, since most elementary schools lack libraries and since a wide variety of services are being provided to elementary schools by public libraries. It was assumed that all the secondary schools would have a library, and they all did. It could be expected that in the whole suburban area surrounding Chicago there would be communities where the total provision of materials would be representative of most of the areas of our country, except for the strictly rural regions.

It was obvious that on the perimeter of this city there are suburbs in all degrees of development, ranging from the large, long-established community with considerable wealth and many cultural and intellectual centers to the small, very new community with few resources in finances and overwhelmed with problems of rapidly increasing population.

These twenty-seven communities are served by fifteen high schools and fifteen public libraries, all but one of which are tax-supported. Eight public libraries are located in communities under 25,000. Size of public library collections to serve the entire population ranges from the two largest, long-established collections of 185,000 and 109,000, to three between 7,000 and 8,000, the median being 27,000. Book budgets range from $25,000 and $27,000 to $214, with the median at $6,800. In three communities the total number of volumes in the high-school library is greater than in the public library collection, and in four cases the book budgets are higher. This is not surprising, inasmuch as all but three of these communities have experienced very rapid growth in the past ten, and even five, years.

Four patterns of suburban library development can be detected. They are not to be interpreted as exclusive types, but they do represent stages of development.

The first pattern is represented by the large, long-established suburb where relatively little population change has taken place, where there is considerable wealth and only light industry and retail business. Here are located the high schools which have good school libraries, meeting minimum national and state standards in most areas, and surpassing them in some. Here, much experimental work in education is being undertaken. These are the typical "suburban schools," as Dr. Conant uses that term in describing the high schools that heavily emphasize the college-preparatory function.[1] Well-developed public library service has existed for many years, with professional advisory service for children and adults. Book collections are of high quality and, in most cases, adequate in size. Well-selected special collections for young adults are maintained. Although

[1] James B. Conant, *The American High School Today* (New York: McGraw-Hill Book Co., 1959).

there are no specially trained young adult librarians in any of these libraries, service to young people is of high caliber. Magazine collections are good. Except for a few books on closed shelves, there are no restrictions on service to high-school students. At least four of the communities in this survey exhibit this pattern of library service.

It does not follow, however, that these libraries are without any problems in serving high-school students. Particularly heavy demands are made by these students, 80 per cent of whom are college bound, and many of whom are enrolled in accelerated programs. Problems cluster around the usual focus of irritation in school and public library relationships—the term paper and the resultant drain on resources, staff time, and seating space in the public library. Use of periodicals by students is particularly heavy because in two schools the school-library holdings date back to only five years. The reported frequent use of career information in the public library suggests that the school library's excellent collection of such materials is not readily accessible or cannot be used at a time convenient to the students. Or it may reflect a simple preference for the public library because of the opportunity to visit with friends or to browse among the more extensive book collection there available.

The second pattern of community library development is found in suburban communities with a relatively stable population but where there is less wealth represented by owners of large and expensive real estate and where there is more industry, both light and heavy. These communities have spent, through the years, considerably less for both education and libraries than have

other neighboring districts of similar size. This type of community is likely to be engaged in surveys and planning to improve school facilities and programs but is less likely to be concerned at present about the public library.

There are more than four thousand students in public high schools in the two largest of these communities, and at least half that number in parochial schools. For twenty-three hundred students in one of the new high schools the public library is the only source for bound periodicals more than three years old. This library has collections extending back fifteen years of most of the standard magazines, but the facilities for using them consist of less than a dozen tables that occupy the entire adult reading area. Book collections in both public libraries were weak in the subjects of greatest need—in reference material and in up-to-date non-fiction on subjects of current interest and significance. Restriction on free use of collections by high-school readers was evident in both. In one, books on family living, novels which now or in years past excited criticism as to their suitability for the young, including *Grapes of Wrath,* as well as one of the encyclopedias and the college catalogues, were in the librarian's office.

In order to evaluate public library service in the five-community area served by the high school mentioned above, we might consider it in terms of a public library system as formulated in *Public Library Service.* The total population is estimated at slightly above 136,000. The two public libraries serving the two largest communities have one branch each, and one operates a bookmobile. The public library standards conceive of a library system which serves at least 100,000. Such a system should have a minimum of 100,000 titles. The combined holdings of these four libraries is approximately 115,000. Separate titles should be added at the rate of 4,000–5,000 a year, with sufficient duplication to assure the acquisition of one volume for every five persons. To do this, these libraries should be spending about $45,000 for current books and duplicates alone, but their combined budgets for materials total only $24,000. If these libraries were organized as a library system, to meet recommended personnel standards, this would require at least fifteen professionally trained librarians, including librarians trained to give informational and advisory service to young adults and children. In the entire area there are only two profesionally trained librarians in the public libraries.

This is not the time or place to talk about the obvious advantages of the library system in whatever organizational form might be most appropriate to serve an area such as this, but it may be noted that, in spite of bright and attractive public library quarters and alert, interested staffs, there are obviously narrow limits to the total library resources available to high-school students in this large suburban area.

The third pattern of suburban library development is represented by those communities which have experienced very rapid growth in the past decade and which are made up of small dwellings and only light manufacturing and some industrial property. These new communities have developed rapidly and recently from the migration out of central city areas of transition. Planning lags behind building, schools are new and quickly overcrowded, with resources therefore at a minimum, but there is a growing consciousness of community needs and a developing citizen responsibility. Public library services either are likely to be non-existent or are developing in a somewhat haphazard and stop-gap character to meet the obvious need felt by adults accustomed to such services in the city.

As an example of the problems posed by new suburbs of this type we may examine one such group on the southern edge of the city. The area included is roughly 6 miles by 12 miles and includes eleven communities. Total estimated population is 100,000, and it has almost doubled since 1950. Three of these communities are above 18,000 in population; one of the smaller suburbs has increased to two and a half times its 1950 population. There is every evidence that this pattern of growth will continue, as the movement of industry to the southern suburbs has been increased by construction of the Calumet Sag Canal. Within this area there are two four-year, one junior-senior, and two freshman-sophomore high schools. All but one have been built in the last five years. Most students ride to school in busses, the proportion ranging from 90 per cent in one school to 50 per cent in another. In two of the schools only 20 per cent are college bound. An estimate of 50 per cent is reported for a third school. Many students in the upper grades hold jobs, and early dropouts are high. Because of the low college-bound population there is limited homogeneous grouping; but four languages are taught in two of the three school systems, and special provision for reading instruction, as well as for accelerated classes in mathematics, is generally made.

What are the resources in library materials and services available to the 5,700 high-school students enrolled in the public schools of the area? Each of the five school libraries has adequate seating space, although one library cannot quite accommodate 10 per cent of the enrolment. The quarters in all are attractive, with adequate lighting and functional furniture. Personnel is of high professional competence but averages only one per 1,100 students. Book collections average 5.2 books per pupil, the range being from 8 to 2.6. Budgets for the coming year for books, periodicals, pamphlets, and binding average $2.90, with a spread from $2.25 to $5.00. These allotments are less adequate than they seem, since all but one of the libraries have existed five years or less and are still engaged in building basic collections.

In this same area there are three public libraries which are tax-supported. The largest library has a collection of 22,000 books serving 18,000 people and open forty-six hours a week, with a book budget of $1,343. The second largest library's collection numbers 16,000, to serve a population of 22,000; the building is open thirty-three hours a week. Fifty per cent of the collection consists of children's books, and they account for 75 per cent of the circulation; there are no elementary-school libraries in the community. The book budget amounts to $4,358. The third library contains only 7,000 volumes, and the book budget is $214. This library is open twenty-six hours a week. The collection shows the evidence of a heavy dependence upon gifts, particularly on the shelves of children's books. All three libraries are staffed by a minimum number of persons, none professionally trained. Service is limited to providing and circulating as many books as the budget permits. This pattern of library development is typical

of the new suburbs where there has been rapid growth, building of schools with barely adequate facilities, and where no tax funds are available for a public library. In these communities, as in those mentioned earlier, a form of co-operative service to provide professional public library services would be the answer; however, the trend is for each village to build its own library before appointing the librarian.

But where in this whole area is a student to go for, say, a magazine article from a 1938 periodical? Neither school nor public library is keeping magazines beyond five years, because of recency of building, and not all the schools have them back even to that date. In one case the school librarian is helping the public library to develop a collection that dates back only two years. Where is the high-school reader to find books on a special subject field or a collection of more sophisticated dimensions than one geared to the *Standard Catalog for High Schools* or the *Basic Book Collection for High Schools*? Where are interested young parents to find professional guidance in building a child's first experiences with literature? Where is a young person to find a public library collection which contains not only older children's books but a challenging selection of adult books appropriate for young people and a trained young adult librarian to guide him? This young person may be the gifted student, or he may be the reluctant reader with needs that call for rich resources. This suggests what we mean by the public library complementing the school library. This is not a luxury service; this is minimum essential service to achieve educational objectives.

In the case of the high-school students in this area (and remember there are 5,700 of them in public schools alone), those who are fired with sufficient enthusiasm and initiative seek material beyond the basic reference books at the nearest branch of the Chicago Public Library. This branch has had a large increase in the use of its collection by students in the past ten years, and a large part of that increase has come from suburban residents. Circulation has increased until this branch which was once a medium-size branch (100,000 circulation per year) has grown to become one of the largest branches, with an annual circulation of 232,000. Since there is only one elementary-school library in this suburban area, a constantly increasing use of the children's books and of the senior collection, which is used through the ninth grade, has given this branch the fifth highest children's circulation in the city. The largest population growth has been not within the city limits but in the adjoining suburbs. Librarians report the overcrowding of the library at term-paper time to be serious. For the students this sometimes means traveling considerable distance, and it means that either they or a member of their family must be eligible for a Chicago Public Library card.

A fourth pattern of library service has developed in a community which is unique in many respects—that of Park Forest, a planned community south of Chicago which has grown from a village of 8,000 to one of an estimated 30,000 in ten years. It is a village of individually owned homes, plus a few areas of rental units; it consists of middle-income families, with a high percentage of heads of families in professional and business careers. It is a community highly conscious of its cultural needs, and good educational and recreational facilities have been in the planning from the beginning. These are being achieved with both forward and backward steps. The first elementary school had an elementary library, but this was lost early as the need for classrooms crowded it out. The junior high school operates without a library, but the high school which serves a township enrolment of 1,450 has a high-school library adequate in space, with two librarians, and a small collection of approximately 7,000 books. The library is a materials center with a fairly good collection of audio-visual materials but little by way of pamphlets, and it has only minimum holdings of periodicals. Obviously, such a community, with 90 per cent of its students college bound, and with a special program for the academically talented, makes heavy demands on library resources. The public library has been in existence only about five years, and one year ago was moved into a new building, paid for by a bond issue to build the first third of the building. The library was outgrown the week it opened in terms of public use. An excellent collection of books built by a highly experienced professional librarian has received phenomenal use. This library ranks tenth in the state in circulation, though only fifty-second in book collection and twentieth in salary budget. It is first in the state in circulation per dollar. It is readily apparent that here is a situation where real pressure is exerted by 1,450 high-school students highly motivated in an enriched curriculum; a school collection which provides not quite five books per pupil and almost no magazine files extending back more than five years is not good enough. At that, the high school students are better served than are the elementary and junior high pupils. All the irritating problems mentioned earlier are present in the public library. Tables and chairs are filled every school night by high-school and junior high school students doing reference work on school assignments. Book lists from teachers who have not checked availability are often too short and seem never to have provided for substitutions. Teachers in the junior high and elementary schools want to bring classes for instruction in use of the library and reference tools. High-school students want materials not available in the high-school library and never available in sufficient quantities at one time: novels by Faulkner, Hemingway, Thomas Wolfe, and other modern writers; literary criticism, American history studies, and reference sources. Part of the trouble lies in a high-school library collection where there has been too heavy reliance on selection from basic selection aids. As an example, there is one title by Steinbeck, *The Pearl*.

This is a community where the public librarian has taken steps to establish relationships to make for more harmonious service. First steps were negative: high-school students were not permitted to reserve books and were allowed to borrow only two books on a subject. Positive steps were taken in meetings arranged with the members of the library board, the superintendent of schools, and representatives of the school board, and with the curriculum director for the elementary schools. The schools recognized the need to hire a consultant for the elementary grades, and it is planned to hire a junior high librarian. The curriculum co-ordinator plans a series of talks by the public librarian to teachers in a workshop on instructional materials and their most

effective use. The high-school librarian is suggesting one change which is becoming increasingly obvious as a possible solution—that of opening the high-school library several evenings during the week.

A new high school for the township, a branch of the present school, is to be built a few miles away in an adjacent suburb; and the superintendent, in forecasting the needs of the community, asked the question that is being asked in other new communities and for which each school and public librarian must prepare an answer: Why should we have two libraries, why not one library located in the school but serving the public? Librarians may recognize that, as Lowell Martin has said, locating public library branches in schools proved to be an ill-fated experiment.[2] We may hope, therefore, that this practice has been abandoned. Nevertheless, the question is still being raised in communities, and I venture to predict that it will continue to appeal to many administrators and taxpayers as a workable solution.

The survey of library resources for young people in suburban Chicago led to certain observations applicable to all communities; they form the basis for the following conclusions.

A problem which seemed to be common to most of the school libraries in the area was the provision of printed materials other than books. A good selection of magazines was available, but there was less representation of the serious adult magazines than would appear necessary.

Pamphlet collections were at a minimum, except for vocational pamphlets.

[2] Lowell Martin, "Relation of Public and School Libraries in Serving Youth," *A.L.A. Bulletin*, LIII (February, 1959), 113.

Only two schools had acceptable collections. Quantitative standards for pamphlet collections cannot reasonably be established. True, the need for such material depends upon teachers' use, but it is no less true that the librarian can use her professional knowledge to aid teachers. The librarian has the specialized knowledge and opportunity to put her skills and knowledge at the service of the teacher in adding dimensions to her class program—dimensions that the average teacher has little opportunity to be aware of otherwise—but this service is not possible if the school librarian never gets out from behind the desk. Curriculum administrators are calling for organized channels to inform teachers about all areas of instructional materials and are speaking of needs for new publications and new bibliographies. These are aids that would not be needed if school librarians were doing their job. In this one area of pamphlets the librarian can provide leadership in gathering resource material. In social studies—notably world geography—in science, in local history and government, the pamphlet quite often is all that we can provide, but the fact that the material is ephemeral does not excuse the failure to make it available; this factor underscores the need to gather the only resources available.

The absence of really rich resources in pamphlet collections reflects less the inadequacy of book budgets than it does the shortage of personnel. Selecting and processing pamphlets is a time-consuming task. In two area schools surveyed, one librarian serves 1,000 students, and one serves 1,700. Even with the part-time clerical help available, there is not likely to be time for the selection needed to develop more than a minimum file of pamphlets. In

only two schools was there evidence of duplication of reference material for circulation to classrooms or homes.

In the larger and long-established communities, there are fewer reports from public libraries of serious pressures from heavy use of materials and facilities by high-school students, but, where they do exist, they are the same problems that plague libraries of all sizes: no notification from teachers of advance assignments, and students overflowing the available adult reference and reading-room space. More often, however, in the larger libraries there is communication, at least to some degree, between the staffs of the two institutions. In one suburb there is considerable informal book-selection consultation and sharing of information and tools. The school librarian is a frequent visitor to the public library, to borrow materials and to seek and give information. The public librarian visits the school less often. At least two communities reported the sharing of display materials. One library sponsors a book fair jointly with the elementary schools, and other special community book programs have involved all librarians in the community.

In the areas where public libraries are less well developed, there was no evidence of co-operation, even on an informal level. The extent of communication seemed to be to return books found in the wrong library. It may be that school librarians are less ready than might be hoped to assume responsibility for solving the problem of resources on a community-wide basis.

Obviously, the lengthening of the school hours of service, including evening hours, is an important development, where the facilities are available in the school but not accessible because of schedules in the school day, or because of other limiting factors. If this practice is to be followed in the future, school libraries must be planned with this in mind. The library on an upper floor at the end of a long corridor cannot be made readily accessible at night. This will be one of the problems to keep in mind in consulting with administrators and architects concerning improved facilities.

The extent of the use of central city reference rooms and specialized library collections by students suggests the desirability of regional information control centers, making use of new developments in telephonic and television communication. Area planning for the extension of library information services should be a co-operative undertaking by school and public library.

In considering the total resources of a community, the school librarian should look beyond those in the immediate environment and refer the student who is capable of and ready for serious research to materials in university and special collections and in the state library. Obviously, research in a university library is not for every high-school student, even if the university could take care of them, but for the young person with well-developed habits of study and for whom the chance to investigate a subject of interest more intensively than either school or public library can allow, the new horizons of a university or special collection may present unlimited possibilities. The Chicago metropolitan area has a number of such collections. The University of Chicago reference librarians reported that four to six high-school students asked for help every Saturday during the school year and that at least half

of them were from schools other than the University High School. The John Crerar Library of Science, Technology, and Medicine had some interesting figures in a survey of reader use in September, 1958. During the preceding year high-school students had accounted for a little under 4 per cent of the total use of volumes from the stacks. Ninety high schools were represented among the users of the John Crerar Library, and at least half of them were suburban high schools.

In the well-developed curriculums of today's schools, students are being stimulated and guided to work at their highest level of performance. One aspect of their learning is to acquire the habit and skill of using many sources and of checking their reliability. To offer a gifted student the resources of a fine reference collection and to guide him in its use is to give him the best possible opportunity for enriched learning. Ways must be found to make these materials accessible to the capable high-school students without jeopardizing the function of the special research libraries in the education of adults and in services to their specialized clientele. It is a problem to be solved in each area by the school librarians and the university or special librarians. Controls agreed upon should not be in the nature of prohibitions but for the purpose of screening the serious student with a well-defined problem ready for research. The school librarian should lay the foundation before the need arises so that she can make arrangements for use by students and faculty of special library resources in the community.

One aspect of co-operative relationships which is frequently discussed in theory but which never appeared in actuality in this survey was that of duplication of materials. There is obviously no need for mutual concern over the possibilities of duplication; we need more, not less, duplication. It is possible that the storing or microfilming of some periodicals could profitably be planned co-operatively, although even here the issues of recent years are in demand from all segments of the library's public, and many copies of these publications could be used. It is important for the school librarian to know about the specialized reference materials that are available in the public library so that students may be referred to them; however, this is not done in order to avoid duplication. School libraries should find out what subject areas are being used most heavily in the public library by students and should duplicate titles on these bibliographies for the high-school library. Informed book-buying for high-school students will lead to more duplication, but it will be planned for maximum use and will at all times be a co-operative activity.

In like manner the public librarian needs to visit the school library and examine shelves and consult bibliographies to find out what texts are being used and what resource units followed. The word "textbook" should cease to be the "naughty word" that it has become to public librarians. Modern textbooks in science, in the social studies—especially history—and in many other areas are exceedingly useful reference tools, and a variety of them on the shelves would add to the informational sources for all readers.

There is a rich field for more formal co-operation in the process of selection. This is an established pattern of procedure in large city systems where school and public librarians serve together on book-evaluation committees to the profit of both; there is even greater need for it in the small and medium-sized communities where librarians have less access to books, less money to spend, and a great need to make each dollar count.

It has been the fashion at this conference to engage in considerable crystal-ball gazing—or, more accurately, to analyze trends and to forecast the shape of school libraries to come. The crystal ball is more clouded when I look into it. When the new school has been built, supplied adequately with materials and staffed by enough trained specialists in instructional materials, then the public library staff—children's librarians and young adult librarians—will be free to explore new patterns of service, to devise new definitions, no longer being tied to unwieldy school service collections and programs of school visiting. There is today, however, a discouragingly vast separation in understanding and a great absence of communication. Children's librarians as a whole are woefully ignorant of educational goals and methods and rejoice in this state with a misplaced pride. Knowledge of the way curriculums are developed and of the psychology of learning is essential to a librarian working with youth anywhere. In the same way, school librarians are ignorant of the role of the public library as an institution serving all the community and of their own stake in it; and this is equally inexcusable.

Possibly, there will be opportunities for defining the role of each profession by recognizing that we have quite definite responsibilities identified with institutions which are distinctly different; paralleling one another in functions at times, but each with a specialized work to do of great importance to the advancement of knowledge. The advancement of the status of librarians working with youth in both school and public libraries will be best served by seeking recognition, not of the likenesses of their patterns of service, but of the significant differences in the programs that give meaning to the role of each institution. Then, perhaps, we will have the necessary perspective to make possible effective relationships, productive of the best in a total library program for all members of the community.

TOWARD EXCELLENCE IN SCHOOL-LIBRARY PROGRAMS

FRANCES HENNE

ONE of the distinct contributions that the United States has made to the education of youth throughout the world is the idea of the school library. The ministries of education in many countries have demonstrated interest in the study and application of the principles of school-library programs as developed in this country. In our own schools these same principles are currently receiving greater attention and more promotion than ever before from those responsible for the education of children and young people—indeed, to such an extent that, perhaps for the first time in the history of school libraries, talking about achieving excellence in school-library programs holds promise of something more than an academic exercise.

These cheerful words are not meant to blink away the hard truth that the acceptance of the school-library idea has most often been on a level of definition rather than of operation but to recognize that the times are propitious for the establishment and improvement of school libraries. This paper contains, in very brief form, (1) a description of certain socio-educational factors that uphold the need for excellence in school library programs; (2) a consideration of some obstacles that have hindered or retarded school-library programs in reaching their fullest potentialities; and (3) a notation of those areas in school librarianship that seem to hold the greatest promise for facilitating the achievement of excellence and therefore require the most immediate action.

I

Many, if not most, of the elements that create an extremely favorable climate for school libraries today are not basically new in concept; the newness comes in the widespread interest directed toward them and in an increasing willingness to do something about them. Of the eleven socio-educational developments selected for mention, the following five have been particularly influential for many years in effecting the provision and betterment of library resources and services in schools.

1. The improvement of schools, higher standards in the objectives of elementary and secondary education, and enrichment in the content and design of curriculums have continuously amplified the use made of school-library resources by students. The place of the school library, as a fundamental part of the school, has thus come about naturally and not through artificial or superimposed measures; it has grown from and been shaped by those basic principles that determine the content and method of the best education for all children and young people. The statement that a school is as good as its library is not an idle one; and the request always made by a well-known educator when asked to plan curricular improvements in a school—"First, let me see your library"—highlights the essential character of the library in the instructional program of the school.

2. Imaginative, stimulating, and effective teaching has always motivated students to use a wide range of library

75

resources and has depended for best results on an abundance of books and other materials being easily accessible in the school. As creative teaching, the expansion of knowledge, and educational changes have made textbook-dominated teaching obsolete, the collections of the school library have become indispensable. Neither the requirements of good teaching nor the intellectual curiosity and imagination of children and young people can be satisfied with a single textbook, or with sets of books, or with limited school-library resources.

3. Over the years the great increase in the student population has meant an ever widening demand to provide for the many individual differences that exist among students in reading, learning, and personal development. To meet these rightful claims of children and young people requires a wide range of books and other materials.

4. With the expansion of knowledge and the rapid change in many of its fields, a wide range of library materials has long been essential in the school. New developments must be reflected in the content of the curriculum and in the breadth of range and up-to- dateness of the library resources available for students and teachers. Since the domains of knowledge and experience have become too extensive to be covered even remotely within the scope of classroom teaching, the school library has become much more than a collection of resources for curricular purposes. It is more, too, than a source of materials for special interests, hobbies, and leisure-time pursuits, important though these are. Through the program and collections of the school library, ideas, knowledge, and aesthetic experiences are introduced, stimulated, and fostered. Materials of all types, imaginative and

factual, and in all forms, printed and audio-visual, serve to animate the many interests of youth. For research and inquiry motivated by classroom instruction, for the acquisition of information and knowledge sparked by personal interest and curiosity, and for the stimulation of exploration in unknown fields, the school library is one of the most important, as well as one of the most exciting, single elements in the education of the child and young person; it is a source of wisdom, information, experience, enjoyment, good taste, and wonder.

5. The discipline of knowing how to use the resources of a library intelligently has always been important in the education of youth, not only as a skill necessary for success in schoolwork and other activities, but also as a type of knowledge needed for later use in adult life. Today, the ability to use a library and its resources is one of the major rudiments of education, and not merely for the collection of materials or for the location of facts to satisfy the requirements of class assignments. The critical analysis and evaluation of materials and judgment and reflection regarding the use of their contents form part of the educational process that teaches students to be thinking people. The currently emphasized objective of schools to develop the students' abilities for self-directed learning depends upon a library and its resources as the key instrument in this process. "Self-directed learning" may be a pedagogic term, but it nonetheless represents one of the most important attributes to be acquired by children and young people in their education, and it constitutes the basic ingredient in shaping the attitude, interest, and ability for the ongoing process of education that continues through a

lifetime. Never before has so much substantive content learned in the classroom become obsolete so soon or has the need been so acute for members of a well-informed, rational society to make continuous use of the sources of knowledge, of which a library is a major one. The teaching program and the resources of the school library are vital for these aspects of the school's instructional program.

The above developments reflect some of the important reasons that have shaped the objectives and functions of school libraries over a considerable length of time. During recent years they have become increasingly significant, and, the school-library program has grown in stature, scope, and significance. Today, there are additional socio-educational forces in existence that have many implications for the improvement of school libraries. One, of course, is the very live and widespread interest among citizens in providing quality education for all children and young people and in the active participation of citizen groups in effecting improvements in the schools. Closely allied is the current upheaval in the evaluation of education, accompanied by a series of publications that are exerting considerable influence and instigating serious and lively discussions. Although not all the authors of these works have mentioned or stressed the school library, what they recommend for the improvement of education, divergent though their approaches may be, depends in large measure on abundant library resources and active school library programs being available in the school.[1]

The curricular changes and instructional innovations that are now being discussed or put into practice emphasize the use of the school library: ungraded elementary schools, individualized instruction, variations in size of classroom areas and of class groups, homogeneous ability groupings in subject areas, advanced and accelerated programs, and others.

Another noteworthy development is an interest in the school library observable in the activities of citizen groups, at both national and local levels, and in the professional organizations of school administrators, curriculum co-ordinators, and classroom and special teachers. We are currently witnessing a spate of meetings, projects, and publications, either completed by these groups or in the planning stage, that center on school-library services and resources. The leadership and support that is today coming from within these citizen, administrative, and teaching groups constitutes a major step in the move-

[1] Among these writings are: Francis S. Chase and Harold A. Anderson (eds.), *The High School in a New Era* (Chicago: University of Chicago Press, 1958); James B. Conant, *The American High School Today* (New York: McGraw-Hill Book Co., 1959); National Education Association, *The Identification and Education of the Academically Talented Student in the American Secondary School* (Washington, D.C.: National Education Association, 1958); American Association of School Administrators, *The High School in a Changing World: 36th Yearbook* (Washington, D.C.: National Education Association, 1958); Educational Policies Commission, *An Essay on Quality in Public Education* (Washington, D.C.: National Education Association, 1959); National Association of Secondary-School Principals, *Images of the Future,* ed. J. Lloyd Trump (director, Commission on the Experimental Study of the Utilization of the Staff in the Secondary School) (Washington, D.C.: National Education Association, 1959); Rockefeller Brothers Fund, *The Pursuit of Excellence: Education and the Future of America* ("America at Mid-Century Series," Special Studies Project Report V [Garden City, N.Y.: Doubleday & Co., 1958]); Hyman George Rickover, *Education and Freedom* (New York: E. P. Dutton & Co., 1959); and Alexander J. Stoddard, *Schools for Tomorrow: An Educator's Blueprint* (New York: Fund for the Advancement of Education, 1957).

ment toward excellence in school-library programs. The participation of representatives from these groups in the formulation and implementation of the new national standards for school libraries has been of inestimable value.

This awareness of the school-library program and the keen interest in instructional materials of all kinds, plus the realization that the school library is an integral part of the school, has probably contributed to another significant development—an increase in the number of schools and departments of education recognizing that instruction about books, other materials, and library services for children and young people must be incorporated in the professional preparation of teachers. These agencies, too, are becoming increasingly interested in the close relationship that exists between the professional education of teachers and of school librarians.

Finally, in this very brief listing of developments that are helping to shape an environment conducive to excellence in school-library programs, the new national standards for school libraries have a place. Even before their appearance in print, the standards, through the several preliminary editions that have been released and through innumerable meetings and conferences focusing on their content and purpose, have brought the importance of quality in school-library programs very much into the foreground, and they have created an awakened interest in this subject throughout the country. The standards are timely and useful, providing a planning guide desired by many schools. The phrase "toward excellence" is particularly appropriate for the standards, since their immediate goals are the very good school-library programs that, for innumerable schools in this country, cir-

cumstances dictate must first be reached before achieving real excellence.

In this discussion we have observed that significant socio-educational trends place emphasis on the importance of library services and resources and that these developments, in conjunction with the interest in improving schools and in providing them with the resources of teaching and learning, have opened many opportunities for the establishment and improvement of school libraries. Working toward excellence therefore means that all individuals interested in and concerned with school libraries must be acutely aware of these developments and must utilize these opportunities at every turn. The mere existence of these promising conditions will not automatically improve school libraries; they do encourage the promotion of school-library programs, and this promotion must be assisted by the individual and collective efforts of school librarians and other groups.

II

Working toward excellence in school-library programs also imposes upon us the obligation to appraise past and present achievements and to examine them critically for any implications useful in current and future planning.

The turn of the century is usually cited as the date when the first "modern" school library came into existence. The professional literature dealing with school libraries that appeared during the first quarter of the century reveals that the objectives of school libraries during that period had much in common with those of today. Fifteen years ago, when the first compilation of national standards appeared, the principle that good school programs require good school libraries had been clearly demonstrated and widely accepted. Several developments in the social and educational scheme had made it imperative for the good school to have a wide variety of library resources easily accessible to students and teachers and to have the library staff, facilities, and program necessary for the effective selection and use of these materials. During the last fifteen years there have been steady gains in improvements in the school-library field. Among the more noteworthy examples are the development of national, state, and local standards for school libraries, the expansion and vitalization of school-library programs, an increase in the number of city, county, and state school-library supervisors, and a growth in the number of elementary-school libraries, multiple-library situations, centralized technical processing units, and district materials centers.

These advances are important and not to be discounted, but nonetheless it must be admitted that the gains have been made by inches. Although it may sometimes be judicious to accept this relatively slow progress philosophically, it would be ostrich-like optimism if the school-library profession were to view it with either complacency or a belief in its inevitability. For the last fifteen years, and indeed long before, there have not been twenty-five schools in the country that did not need or could not use better school libraries than they had. Recent educational developments would seem almost to demand excellent school libraries, but these have not been forthcoming. The number of elementary schools without libraries is a national disgrace.

It becomes necessary to think about the current status of school libraries before unloosing rosy platitudes about excellence, for behind this slow growth in the school-library movement must lie the obstacles to be overcome and the challenges to be met on the way toward excellence. It becomes essential to identify and understand these causal factors and then do something about them. Our past efforts have quite evidently been either misdirected or futile or both. Something, surely, must explain the general indifference toward having the resources of teaching and learning in our schools and the seeming rejection on a widespread scale of boks and other materials as basic tools in education.

In what ways have citizens in general and school administrators, teachers, and librarians in particular been responsible for the slow development of school libraries?

School libraries have been earmarked as one characteristic of quality education. The achievement of quality education depends upon the educational adaptability of the school district. "It is the community as a whole, including the school, that is the adapting organism— not the school system alone." In this respect, "some communities are pioneers, some early followers, some late followers, and some laggards." (As far as school libraries are concerned, *"laggard"* would be a courtesy term for many communities; "torpid," "inert," or "motionless" would be more appropriate.) "Regardless of the many legal and social factors which tend to make some schools districts more adaptable than others, the fact remains that adaptability is the product of the action of individuals. Surrounding environment makes adaptability easier or more difficult, but the actual adaptation must be done by people."[2]

When we ask why adaptability has

[2] Paul R. Mort, *Educational Adaptability* (New York: Metropolitan School Study Council, n.d.).

been laggard for school libraries in so many communities, several reasons may be suggested: the anti-intellectualism of a technological democracy and the erroneous identification of libraries with intellectualism; the dependence by adults on mass media for the communication of ideas, information, and entertainment; an unfamiliarity with school libraries (or frequently with any kind of library) in the citizens' own educational and personal experiences; an absence of leadership in the promotion of the school-library idea among citizens (especially true in the case of parents who tend to be favorably responsive to school libraries once they become aware of the services and resources of a good school-library program); a lack of money (not as universally true as is sometimes indicated—witness the great number of schools with colossal gymnasiums, elaborate uniforms and equipment for band members and majorettes, and scanty or non-existent school-library resources and facilities); and, so we are constantly reminded, the inevitable time lag, cultural or otherwise, between the recognition of a worthy educational idea and the translation of that idea into action.[3]

In the case of school administrators, including school-board members, several explanations may be advanced: indifference on the part of some (how else can the absence or the poorly developed

[3] The fifty years that is frequently given as an extreme time span between the introduction and the acceptance of an idea has now lapsed for school libraries. School libraries have been described as being in a pioneer stage for so many years that surely theirs is one of the longest pioneer periods in history, and this writer, for one, is weary of wearing a coonskin cap. It should be stressed that the lag for school libraries is not one between quality and the stage just beneath quality; it is all too frequently the lag between quality and nothing or between quality and what is poor or downright bad.

condition of school libraries in many situations be explained?); the fact that many administrators themselves do not read very much, if at all, and hence do not have an innate belief in or a natural predisposition toward libraries; tendencies to meet pressures for tightening school budgets by reducing the school-library budget because it is administratively more flexible; the restraints imposed by overcrowded schools that result in library space being used for classrooms (this explanation, frequently advanced in the case of elementary schools, is actually an artificial reason but nonetheless a compelling one); a lack of support from the school board or from the community; and an absence of knowledge about good school-library programs due to (a) attending elementary and secondary schools with no library or poor libraries, (b) having received a professional preparation in which school-library resources and programs were not mentioned, and (c) unfortunate impressions created by the library staffs in their own schools or by other librarians.

When we turn to teachers, we again find many contributing factors that explain a lack of interest in school libraries on their part. It is probably true, as some have said, that many teachers have limited cultural backgrounds and do not read very many books. In other cases, teachers who are firm believers in libraries frequently find that they are unable to promote the provision of library resources and services in their schools because of apathy or indifference on the part of their administrative officers. Often those teachers who would be most receptive to learning about books and other materials appropriate for their students and to having the specialized services of librarians regarding instructional materials do not obtain the necessary in-service training and motivation because of lack of leadership on the part of superintendents, principals, curriculum co-ordinators, or librarians. A fundamental weakness again occurs because many teachers have had no experience with good school libraries in their own education; have failed to receive instruction about books, other teaching resources, and library services as part of their professional preparation; have taught in schools with scanty or non-existent library resources; or have been in situations where they did not receive guidance and assistance from school librarians.

Whether textbook-dominated teaching has held sway so long because of the conditions noted above or because of other influences, the fact remains that it has been one of the basic causes in limiting the provision and use of library resources in the schools and also in restricting the horizons of youth.[4]

The group presumably most interested in the development of good school-library programs, the school librarians, has not been without its share of respon-

[4] "Perhaps the most important factor in shaping our attitudes and policies in education is the graded textbook. American schools are predominantly 'textbook' schools. The majority of teachers feel lost without a uniform textbook in the hands of every pupil. Education is conceived by many as a process of memorizing the content of textbooks. Limited goals are set in terms of the content of textbooks. Examinations are based upon the content of textbooks. Educational progress is measured in terms of pages covered in the textbook, and the intellectual ability required for success at a given grade level or in a given subject is determined by the textbook. The basic assumption underlying textbook procedure is that pupils can be classified into homogeneous groups and taught uniform material by a standardized procedure. The textbook has a place in education, but these assumptions inhibit the process of making 'schooling' truly educational" (Walter W. Cook, "The Gifted and the Retarded in Historical Perspective," *Phi Delta Kappan*, March, 1958, pp. 249–50).

sibility in slowing the progress of school libraries. Many morals may be drawn from the mores of school librarians, of which only a few can be noted here. An unawareness of new developments in education and in school librarianship has too often been evidenced by school librarians and has frequently resulted in failures to make significant progress even when the opportunities have been at hand. Closely related is the persistence that many have in clinging to the same emotional responses to the "controversial" issues of old, even though changes in time, in schools, and in libraries have completely altered the complexion of these subjects. On too many occasions we have confused the value of an idea or rejected it entirely, not in terms of the worth of the idea, but in relation to the circumstances that at the moment may make its introduction or implementation difficult.

In the next section of this paper the importance of having adequate staff for school libraries will be stressed. Tradition and historical accident have exerted too great an influence in keeping school libraries from having staffs, both professional and clerical, that are large enough to put full-scale programs into operation. The image of the school librarian as a handmaiden or willing martyr may have its roots in virtue and in commendable zeal, but two elements that have shaped this image have, in the final analysis, rendered disservice to the progress of school libraries—the faiure on the part of many school librarians to request staff assistance that is legitimately needed for their school-library programs and the extensive amount of free, overtime work that they have spent in the school and in the home on library matters (in addition, that is, to what is defined as legitimate "homework" for school librarians). The continuation and expansion of the unpaid student assistant program in school librarians, with an almost foolhardy lack of recognition that this program was originally conceived as a makeshift for obtaining additional help that was critically needed, has hindered school libraries from obtaining a full complement of professional and clerical staff members. (This situation is not without its irony inasmuch as a sound educational program for student assistants, which under appropriate circumstances has a place in many school-library programs, adds to the librarian's work load rather than diminishing it.) Today, the nature of the curricular programs of students in many junior and senior high schools is tending to reduce or to eliminate student library-assistant activities, and this trend may bring about a much needed re-evaluation of the total situation regarding student library assistants.

The unwitting dissemination on the part of some school librarians of the impression that anyone can do school-library work has on numerous occasions had unfortunate outcomes in the opinions that school administrators, teachers, and others have formed of the nature of professional library work, and it has also discouraged provision of qualified library staff members in sufficient number. This impression has been created by the student assistant program, by the willing acceptance of having parents and other volunteers staff school libraries (particularly in elementary schools), by the tendency of librarians to compress library-school courses into their teaching of children and young people the use of the library and its resources, and by the too elastic rationalization of the premise that something is better than nothing, even though that

something is distinctly non-professional.

It would be unfortunate if the above parade of negative circumstances were to be interpreted as being universally true, as lacking cognizance of the notable contributions made by many citizens, school administrators, teachers, and school librarians, or as being a series of damning statements made with no purpose other than their mere utterance. Even the brief analysis presented here of some causal factors tending to retard progress in the school-library field provides suggestions for areas of concentration in immediate planning programs that have working toward excellence in school-library programs as their goal. These areas are discussed in the following section of this paper.

III

To isolate certain areas as being key ones in a program of action directed toward achieving excellence in school-library programs is always a subjective and highly selective process. The points that have been selected for discussion in this paper in no way constitute a comprehensive survey of needed developments in the school-library field. The new national standards for school-library programs present goals for library resources and services in all types of school and thereby can serve as a blueprint for national planning for school libraries. Some extremely important areas for development that are emphasized in the standards merit full discussion but can only be listed here: the provision of libraries in all schools having two-hundred or more students (a long-established standard that always brings to mind the starved library conditions of most of our elementary schools and the efforts and planning that must be directed toward establishing libraries in elementary schools through-out the country), making library serv-ices and resources available for schools having fewer than two-hundred stu-dents, the provision on state and local levels of the services of school-library supervisors or co-ordinators, and the establishment of materials centers. In this paper seven points have been se-lected as representing critical problems requiring the immediate attention of in-dividual school librarians, the school-li-brary profession, and library schools (that other individuals, groups, and agencies are involved and share respon-sibility for the solution of these prob-lems is implied in the discussion). These points do not have equal significance, but each is important in an over-all de-sign for the improvement of school-li-brary programs.

1. One of the most critical problems in the field of school librarianship is that of obtaining for the individual school a qualified library staff (professional and clerical) that is sufficiently large to con-duct a complete and effective school-li-brary program. Talking about increas-ing the size of the library staff so that the values of dynamic school-library programs can be fully shown may be received with hollow laughter by most school librarians, and it is fully admit-ted that mere words contribute little to improving the general situation. Never-theless, meeting standards recommend-ed for the number of staff members is the key element in demonstrating the true worth of school libraries and their contributions to the education of youth, and it requires the deliberation and ef-forts of the librarian in the school and of the national, state, and local profes-sional groups of school librarians.

With relatively few exceptions, the school libraries of this country consist of one-librarian libraries, a prevailing condition that affects almost any prob-lem in the school-library field that can be mentioned. A complete library program cannot be implemented without suffi-cient staff, and the absence of this dem-onstration has exerted influence on the attitudes of many school administrators about the needs and services of school libraries. The image of the overworked school librarian keeps young people from entering the profession, and not infre-quently school librarians change to other professional fields because of the ardu-ous demands of their impossible work-loads. A lack of time to do comprehen-sive and intensive selection of books and other materials has retarded the prog-ress of the establishment of district ma-terials centers. The professional educa-tion of school librarians has been geared toward the one-librarian library, with some dire results. The development of national professional strength has been affected in that the one librarian can-not get away to meetings, is often too tired to taken an interest in anything beyond the job at hand, and suffers from not having the many benefits that accrue from mutual discussions of prob-lems and practices in the field. Promis-ing developments in school-library pro-grams can rarely move beyond the dis-cussion stage, so dependent are they on staff in sufficient number—extended hours of service during the school year and summer programs, for example. Even more unfortunate is the reality that major and vital parts of any good school-library program cannot be done fully or undertaken at all–frequent, sometimes daily, conferences with all teachers about books and other materi-als for their classes and about library services they would like for themselves, for individual students, and for class groups; individual work with students in the school library in relation to reading, instruction in the use of library resources, and informal teaching of many kinds; the modest guidance program that belongs to every teacher in the school, including school librarians. Some of the stipulations of current library programs come from exigencies arising from libraries being understaffed rather than from any proved philosophy—curtailing services to individual students in locating and assembling books and other materials for their assignments or other purposes, requiring teachers always to accompany their class groups when they come to the library, and similar measures. As for some recently advanced ideas that merit experimentation and demonstration—for example, having library staff members become materials specialists in designated subject areas, or in junior and senior high schools having each professional member of the school-library staff teach one class in a subject area (the subjects to vary among the staff) so that close identification with the curriculum can be established—these are literally impossible without a staff of adequate size.

The national standards make recommendations concerning the size of the library staff that is needed for active and effective library programs. These recommendations are for very good school-library programs, and they constitute an important element in achieving excellence in school libraries. Even so, and as noted in the standards, the recommendations for staff size do not allow the librarians very much time to give weekly to each student and teacher in the school if their schedules were to consist only of work with these individuals, and less time when their schedules include those activities that are typically a continuous part of the librarian's program—the selection and acquisition of materials, group work, and related services. The realization of this fact in itself should be sufficient to counter any glib pronouncement that the standards for size of staff are visionary. Other analyses would also lend support to having more professional and clerical assistance than we now commonly have in school libraries: records of what librarians cannot do to meet needs and requests of students and teachers because of lack of time due to understaffing; job analyses showing the percentage of time spent by the librarian in clerical work, in housekeeping duties, in technical processing, in work with teachers and students, and in other activities; and records of the amount of unpaid overtime spent in work that legitimately should be performed during the regular working day. Comparisons between the size of staff now found in school libraries and those in the libraries of junior colleges and four-year liberal arts colleges are illuminating and telling; to make these comparisons is neither far-fetched nor illogical, since the demands made on the staff in an active school-library program are as heavy, if not more so, as in college libraries. *Toward* excellence means achieving the national standards for staff in school libraries; *excellence* means surpassing them.

2. An equally critical problem in school librarianship is that of improving the professional education of school librarians. It is of course obvious that no professional education is completed when the diploma is grasped in hand and that, in a very true sense, real education begins with work experiences. Nevertheless, the growing interest in and concern about the initial prepara-

tion of those planning to work with the resources of teaching and learning in schools have many implications for developing in greater degree in the professional education of school librarians the specialized competencies that they need. This topic is a large and complex one, and it is always hazardous to select a few points for emphasis without discussing them in relation to the complete context of professional education. It is true that there have been changes and improvements in the professional preparation of school librarians during the last twenty years and that this field has been recognized as an area of specialization within library education; but, in the main, these developments have been rather conservative in nature.

The socio-educational conditions noted in the beginning of this paper that make the times auspicious for the improvement of library resources and services in schools have also contributed to fostering, among curriculum, teaching, audio-visual, and library groups, a deep interest in the professional preparation of instructional materials specialists. That the general area of instructional materials represents a field of specialization or departmentation in itself and one that can be most profitably developed by joint planning between schools or departments of education and those of library service has been recognized fairly extensively in theory but only spottily established in performance. There is evidence, however, of action and exploration regarding the definition and implementation of this specialized area program. The over-all term of instructional materials (or some equivalent designation) for this area is comprehensive in nature, so that varying degrees of specialization can be provided for and so that different groups of students can be reached. A fully developed program would direct the professional education of school librarians and audio-visual materials specialists and would include the content in this specialized field needed in the preparation of classroom and special teachers, curriculum co-ordinators, and others. (Students from all these groups would be enrolled in some basic, elementary courses of common interest and need.) For students specializing in the area program, courses in related fields of education, library science, and other subjects would form part of their professional preparation.

Whether this area program is administered jointly by schools (or departments) of education and schools (or departments) of library service or by other administrative measures depends upon local policies and organizational patterns, but this close affiliation of students specializing in instructional materials, on the one hand, and the agencies responsible for their professional preparation, on the other, needs to be established and maintained. The professional training of school librarians must be identified with that of teachers, since the school librarian is a special teacher in the school. Whether the methods for preparing teachers today are good or indifferent, the library profession must recognize them as the basic pattern for the preparation of school librarians and participate in improving the quality of teacher education. Many new proposals and experiments in the education of teachers have seldom reached even a discussion stage as far as their implications for the preparation of school librarians are concerned, and, to say the least, this has been unfortunate. It is not enough to bring about this identification of school librarians with the preparation of teachers through the channel of certification requirements. A total, carefully planned program is essential. Among many other advantages to be gained, a closer communication and better understanding is developed between propospective school librarians and prospective teachers and administrators.

It is generally agreed that the basic professional education of school librarians has tended to be weak in such areas as curriculum, instructional methods, reading instruction and guidance, and communications and that these essential parts of their preparation should be strengthened. Requiring strengthening, too, is that part of the school librarian's preparation which is the essential core of his specialization—knowledge about the resources of teaching and learning. All prospective school librarians must have, by the end of their basic preparation, an extensive knowledge about the content, selection, evaluation, and uses of books, other printed materials, and audio-visual materials appropriate for children and young people. They must also have similar competencies about textbooks and about professional materials for teachers. School librarians are materials specialists and their initial professional education must prepare them to have the special abilities and types of knowledge that really qualify them as such. Whether the school librarian will or will not administer in his library all types of materials for the school makes no difference. He must know about them and make use of them in his school-library program. School librarians without knowledge of audio-visual materials, or, for that matter, audio-visual specialists without knowledge of books, other printed resources, and library

services, are anachronisms. The degree of excellence to be achieved in the library program of the school depends primarily on this specialized knowledge of the librarians, first acquired in basic professional education, expanded in further specialized and advanced study, and continuously enlarged through experience in the field and the lifetime process of reading, listening, and viewing.

It has been noted that the professional education of school librarians would be centered in the area of instructional materials and that some parts of the basic program would also be taken by classroom teachers and others (children's literature and other materials for children, for example), and it has been implied that a core of specialization would provide the same preparation for those who plan to work with instructional materials in schools (school librarians who have administrative responsibility for audio-visual materials, school librarians who do not have this responsibility, and audio-visual specialists who are connected with a separate department for audio-visual materials). This area program would also permit for "specialization within the specialization," and the time has come when opportunities should be provided for this type of preparation.

We move now into the realms of speculation, and it is difficult to describe in a paragraph or two a subject that requires detailed elaboration. Semantics, the several categories of materials specialists that we have today in schools throughout the country, and the varying patterns of organization for professional education (the undergraduate program, the fifth-year program, and the post–fifth-year program) add to this difficulty. It is assumed that the area program will be a five-year program that may or may not be based on an undergraduate program (this will vary among situations, but under any circumstances fifth-year programs must permit close articulation with undergraduate programs that are soundly planned and have good content). The common core, in part or in entirety, may be taken at the undergraduate level, or it may be completed or taken entirely during the fifth year. In addition to this common core, specialization would seem desirable for the following types of specialized activities in the field: elementary-school librarians, secondary-school librarians, school-libary supervisors, directors or co-ordinators of district materials centers, librarians in charge of centralized technical processing for school-library resources, specialists in the production and use of audio-visual materials and techniques, and faculty members teaching in this area in colleges or universities. Some of this specialization, of course, would incorporate pertinent courses in related areas of library science, education, and the subject disciplines. As school-libary staffs meet and exceed national standards, specialization in the content and materials of various subject disciplines becomes part of the librarian's competency, and the program of professional education must provide for the development of this type of specialization. It is also quite possible that larger school-library staffs may have an impact on the patterns of professional education in another way: gradations in professional training may prove to be quite sensible, and the undergraduate program (with its core of the area program) may serve a real function in the preparation of school librarians for junior positions on school-library staffs.

The idea of an institute for instructional materials with its special area program for school librarians and others working with the resources of teaching and learning, with its own program of demonstration and experimentation, and with its own extensive collection of resources and special equipment is not far-fetched, and there are encouraging signs and activities occurring throughout the country that presage many interesting developments in the near future. That the professional education of school librarians will be reshaped and strengthened seems imminently possible, and with this change prospective school librarians will have not only a broad general education background but specialized knowledge concerning the resources that form the substance of their profession.

3. The inclusion in the professional preparation of teachers of content dealing with library resources and services for the age group that they will be teaching has been advocated for innumerable years. That much remains to be done in this respect is quite evident, even though improvements can be noted that have occurred during the last decade. Immediate developments need not and should not await the creation of the special program described in the preceding paragraphs, since many measures should be undertaken at once in those teacher-training agencies that have not planned this part of the prospective teacher's program. The requirement of courses dealing with books and other materials for children and young people; the inclusion of references to or more detailed content dealing with the functions, services, and needs of school-library programs in the appropriate context of many courses dealing with the curriculum, administration, supervision,

or other aspects of elementary and secondary education; and the availability of excellent demonstration school libraries have long appeared in our professional literature as being minimum basic requirements for prospective teachers and school administrators in the field of instructional materials. These requirements not only form a desirable part of the professional education of teachers but, as noted in the preceding section of this paper, the absence of the types of knowledge and experience that are represented frequently contribute to a lack of understanding of the resources and services of school libraries on the part of teachers, to their subsequent failure to motivate students to use a wide variety of library resources, and to retardation in the establishment, development, and improvement of school libraries. Classroom teachers, desirably, are materials specialists at one level; school librarians, at a more advanced level. Until teachers become acquainted with the materials and services of school libraries as a basic part of their professional preparation, school administrators, school librarians, and school-library supervisors have the responsibility for and the obligation to provide in-service training for teachers about books and other resources of the school library. Urging schools and departments of education to provide for this aspect of teacher education and assisting them in any ways needed are rightful responsibilities of schools or departments of library science, state and local school library professional groups, and school-library supervisors.

4. It is essential for all school librarians to accept the idea of the school library as a materials center as a fundamental part of school-library philosophy and to indicate a willingness to expand the scope of the collections of the school library when the additional funds, staff, and space necessary for their administration and effective utilization are made available. These collections include traditional library resources, audio-visual materials, any supplementary materials for classrooms, and free or rental textbooks. It is recognized that the organization for materials found in some school systems operates on a basis other than a unified administration of these materials, but these instances are relatively few, are usually found only in large systems, and contain many instances where the pattern of split responsibility functions on a system-wide level rather than within the individual schools. It is also recognized that the national association of school librarians has officially indorsed a statement to the effect that the school library is a materials center and that many school librarians have assumed complete or partial responsibility for administering audio-visual materials and textbooks. Nevertheless, a great number of school librarians have resisted extending the scope of the library's collections for purely emotional reasons or because of prejudiced bias, without exerting any effort to explore the possibility of obtaining additional assistance, funds, and facilities for these new collections. No one is recommending that the now grossly overworked librarian add to his heavy load without additional professional or clerical staff or that funds and services for the basic school-library program be reduced. (Sometimes the expansion of the school-library program in these newer directions brings about additional staff and other improvements for the library as a whole when they would not be forthcoming otherwise.)

This point has now been belabored for many years, and the school-library profession has suffered from the painfully slow progress that has been made in this area. The basic theory that all materials must be considered and used in teaching and learning situations and that these materials are frequently supplementary and complementary is so patently sound that having one center for their distribution and use in the school is inevitable. If school librarians do not assume leadership for administering all these materials, it is quite certain that others will. The segmentation of collections of materials in the school into separate organizational units is neither functional nor economical. Particularly in the case of audio-visual materials, the separately administered unit is proving cumbersome and unwieldy for good service. Teachers wish to know all types of materials available on specific subjects and want to obtain information about these materials, as well as the materials themselves, in one place. In good school-library programs, regardless of the pattern under which materials are administered, printed and audio-visual materials of all types are made accessible for use by students and teachers in the library.

5. The topic of "demonstration" is selected here for particular mention, with the realization that all the points preceding and following this one imply or state types of demonstration that are needed in the school-library field. Demonstration can begin in the individual school, and the librarian in the school can do many things to strengthen his own library and thereby the national school-library movement. Again, this is easier said than done, but it seems reasonable to stress once again that the socio-educational factors noted in the first section of this paper and other current developments lend support to an encouragement of school librarians to renew efforts to effect improvements in their own situations. It should be stressed, once more, that these remarks do not have immediate and monumental achievements in mind and that they do attach great value to steady gains made slowly and on a small scale.

There are many parts of the school-library program that are particularly meaningful to educators today and plans for their expansion and improvement have a wider and more receptive audience than heretofore, particularly work with teachers, guiding students in the use of library resources, providing advisory and informational services about books and other materials, participating in the individualized instructional program of the school, and making materials easily accessible for students and teachers.

On the national or regional level, demonstration programs are urgently needed so that administrators, teachers, and librarians may see excellent school libraries in action. (The libraries in demonstration or laboratory schools affiliated with the program of professional education for school librarians and teachers should serve as models in this respect, and those responsible for school libraries of this type have a very real responsibility for assuming leadership in demonstrating school-library programs of excellence.) The few truly excellent school-library programs that we now have need to be made widely known. Filmstrips and films are needed on many aspects of school-library resources and services in the school building, in the school system, and in the state. The establishment of demonstration projects and programs of experimentation is desirable and those being proposed by the implementation committee of the national standards merit full support and encouragement.

The areas for demonstration and experimentation are many: methods for providing library resources and services to very small schools; the organization and services of district and regional materials centers; the uses of bibliographic control and documentation in the analysis and utilization of books and other materials; the effective planning of multiple libraries and other library areas in new building designs for schools; the use of closed-circuit television and new electronic equipment; further exploration in the use of books and other materials to meet the special needs and purposes of teachers and students; the professional education of school librarians; and many others. On many of these topics we have profited from the imagination and enterprise of librarians who have explored and worked successfully in these areas. Library schools have a responsibility for exerting leadership in the implementation of experimentation and demonstration projects. Leadership comes, too, from the national professional organization of school librarians. So important is this organization in all areas that lead to the establishment and improvement of school-library programs that its national strength should be comparable to that of national organizations for classroom teachers and administrators; this pertains to size of member-

ship, to size of staff and funds needed for the work of the association's headquarters, to a wide program of activities, to a professional magazine of stature, and to national conferences that have rich and extensive programs dealing with the resources, services, developments, and problems of school libraries.

6. The implementation of the national school-library standards has already been noted as a measure for providing very good library programs for children and young people. The efforts of school librarians, in co-operation with school administrators, teachers, and others, to help all schools work toward the achievement of these standards contribute, not just to improving libraries or the lot of school librarians, but, most importantly, to the enrichment and quality of the education offered the children and young people of this country.

Good schools, very good schools, and excellent schools all need excellent libraries. Inferior schools need excellent libraries, too, to overcome the omissions of the curriculum and to compensate for the poor instructional program. We accept working "toward excellence in school-library programs" on a pragmatic basis, fully aware of existing realities, of the work ahead, and of the gains that will slowly but surely be made. But, ideally, we know that every child and young person wants, needs, and is entitled to an excellent school-library program.

PRINTED IN U.S.A.